T0380528

THE LIFE-GIVER OF
GENESIS

A Chapter-by-Chapter Study into Who Is God and Who Am I?

DR. ZANE AND RUTH DARLAND

WESTBOW
PRESS®
A DIVISION OF THOMAS NELSON
& ZONDERVAN

WestBow Press books may be ordered through booksellers or by contacting:

WestBow Press
A Division of Thomas Nelson & Zondervan
1663 Liberty Drive
Bloomington, IN 47403
www.westbowpress.com
844-714-3454

ISBN: 979-8-3850-1776-8 (sc)
ISBN: 979-8-3850-1777-5 (hc)
ISBN: 979-8-3850-2306-6 (e)

Library of Congress Control Number: 2024902109

Print information available on the last page.

WestBow Press rev. date: 6/6/2024

To Dr. Phil and Wanda Speas,

This book, *The Life-Giver of Genesis,* is dedicated to you both, with immense gratitude and deep admiration. For thirty years, you have selflessly and generously invested in the lives of Bible College students, leaving an indelible mark on countless hearts.

Your unwavering commitment to humble leadership has served as a shining example of Christ's love and compassion. Through your words, actions, prayer life, and unwavering faith, you have exemplified the essence of the Life-Giver, guiding an entire generation of holiness leaders on their spiritual journey.

Your dedication to the pursuit of knowledge, wisdom, and holiness has inspired all who have had the privilege to learn from you. You have shown us what it truly means to be consumed by the Life-Giver—to live with an unwavering focus on God's grace, mercy, and truth.

Through your guidance and mentorship, you have nurtured young minds and hearts, encouraging them to seek a deeper understanding of God's Word and their own identity in Him. Your investment in the lives of others has borne immeasurable fruit, and the impact of your service will continue to reverberate through generations to come.

In heartfelt appreciation, we thank you, Dr. Phil and Wanda Speas, for your incredible dedication, your unyielding spirit of compassion, and your unfaltering commitment to living a life consumed by the Life-Giver Himself.

CONTENTS

INTRODUCTION
TO GENESIS

Have you ever read the book of Genesis and thought, *What in the world? Did God just say He liked the smell of burning animals? Did God just tell Abraham to murder his son for no reason? Did God want Jacob to have four wives?* The questions are endless. Oftentimes, we end up picking books or verses of the Bible that we can easily understand, and then we ignore the other parts because they seem a little strange. While writing this book, we consulted lots of commentaries and were surprised by how many of the commentaries would skip large sections of verses because they were hard to explain. But God put those strange parts in the Bible for a reason, and He wants us to seek out the truth.

We believe every word of the Bible is true and accurate, but we have chosen to call it a story because it is so important for us to see how the entire Bible is tied together. It isn't just some words of wisdom here, some weird stories there, and then a sweet story of Jesus to top it off. Because the Bible is tied together, it becomes confusing when we pick pieces out of context, and the result is that we form an inaccurate view of God.

The Bible is the story of a big power struggle. God did a stellar job of making a good world. The first page of the Bible tells us over and over that what God did was good. Then, He gave humans the job of managing this good world. What God did on the first page of the Bible was what humans were supposed to keep doing for the rest of the Bible.[1] At this point, the humans had to begin making moral decisions. God gave them lots of power but told them to follow His definition of good and evil. Then, He gave them a chance to prove whether they could do this. A creature in the form of a serpent that is antigod, antihuman, antigood, and antilife came and tempted them. They hijacked God's perfect world.[2]

God waged war on the snake, but He didn't wage war on the humans. God only informed the humans that *now* there would be fear and pain because the giver of goodness and life had been rejected. He told the snake there would be continued hostility between it and the woman and between her seed and its seed.

What does seed mean? We're not talking about plants here. Her seed means the human race, and the snake's seed is the evil with which Satan has infected humans. After giving this warning, God promised a special seed, a special someone, would come and that the evil in people's hearts would bite that special person. That bite will inflict a horrible wound, but in the moment when He is being bitten, this "superman" would crush the snake.[3]

When I (Ruth) was a kid, I remember thinking that God lied to Adam and Eve because they didn't really die. But my thinking was wrong because I already had a concept of the finality of death. Adam and Eve didn't completely die at that moment, but they *began* dying. Before this point, every cell in their bodies continually rejuvenated perfectly. They never had back pain, bad breath, skin blemishes, or sore muscles. Everything about them was fully alive. But that day, the continual rejuvenation stopped, and every cell in their bodies began to die until death consumed them completely.

Have you ever thought, *I like the God of the New Testament but not the God of the Old Testament?* I thought the same thing too until I really started understanding it. Genesis has blown my mind with a more complete picture of who God really is. If you really want to understand Jesus, then allow the God of Genesis to blow your mind too. You may have to set aside your ideas of what the Bible says and allow the Bible to really tell you what is going on. Open your mind and let the Holy Spirit breathe His life and truth into your soul. When we allow ourselves to see God for who He really is, we will begin to realize that He is everything we have ever wanted.

As you read this book, we recommend you start every session in prayer. Together, we're studying God's story, and we need His Spirit to renew and give life to us! Before you begin reading our book, start by reading the Bible chapter first. I (Zane) recommend you get comfortable marking up your Bible with highlights and notations. When something stands out to you, you see connections in the text, or you have a question, mark it! As good as we may think our insights on the flow of the biblical story are, it is more important that you actually read the biblical story for yourself. It is through God's story that He often speaks to us and breathes new life into us. After you've read through the Bible chapter, read through the chapter in this book and take some time to think through the reflection questions. We recommend working through this book with a friend or small group. Using these discussion questions will be a great way to further unpack the Bible's message together, grow deeper in your faith, and solidify what you are learning. With that, let's begin our exciting journey through the story of Genesis!

REFLECTION QUESTIONS:

When you think of Genesis, what thoughts and feelings come to mind?

_____

_____

_____

_____

_____

Whether this is your first time reading through the book of Genesis or your hundredth time, what do you hope to take away from this study?

_____

_____

_____

_____

_____

Jesus tells us in Matthew 18:20, where two or three are gathered, there He is in the midst of them. If you're not already part of a study group, is there someone who could join you in this study of Genesis?

_____

_____

_____

_____

_____

GENESIS 1

The story opens with God making several mind-blowing statements. We cannot handle all of them here, so we'll focus on a few highlights.

Who is this story about? While this first chapter talks about the creation of the world, this chapter is part of one book, which is part of the Bible as a whole. The whole Bible is a story about the Being we call God. The first couple of verses reveal something very dynamic about this Being. The Bible begins by saying that God created the heavens and the earth, but then it says the Spirit was hovering over the waters. So who was there at creation? God or the Holy Spirit? Or both?

God often talks about Himself as both singular and plural.[4] Later in the chapter, God says, "Let Us make man in Our image." This statement lets us know that there was more than one Being present and creating in the beginning. By the time we get to the New Testament, John 1:1 tells us that Jesus was also there and involved in creating the world. With this realization, we recognize there is a whole lot more going on in the creation story. But God knew He was already blowing all our categories, so He just put this teaser in His Word for future reference. Right here, from the beginning, we are given a glimpse of the Trinity. This singular God is plural and in perfect harmony. We have no concept of any relationship that exists in perfect harmony, but here He is. Welcome to the God of Genesis. This is only the beginning!

God then started the work of creating. The initial description of our future home is not appealing. The original Hebrew words tell us that the earth was a dark wasteland covered in deep waters. If I were planning a garden, I wouldn't want to start with a dark desert covered in deep waters! This choice is no accident. God is revealing so much about who He is and what He can do. From the darkness, He produces light. From the chaos, He brings about order. From the barrenness, He generates beauty. These are all amazing things. But the most amazing thing of all was when He created life. God is life. He is all that is good. No situation, person, or environment is so broken that His Spirit cannot breathe life into it. He is a designer with a limitless imagination. He wants His creation to have order and to work in harmony. He desires beauty and structure. He judges and critiques His work because He values what is good.

Let's pause here for a minute. This concept is huge! In a culture that pushes individuality, we often see "good" as something relative we each define for ourselves. However, this simple statement tells us God has already determined what is *good* and what is not. God created a world where goodness is the standard to which all things are held. All of creation will be held accountable if it does not meet this standard. This accountability may sound scary for us because we know we desire and do things that are not good. God is telling us we were initially created good and with a desire for goodness instilled in us. He makes it very clear He delights in harmony and peace within His creation.

What if our Creator enjoyed watching us suffer? The Roman Colosseum was built around AD 70 by an emperor who was considered a "god." He made this structure so people could "enjoy" seeing death and destruction. During the lifetime of the Colosseum, about four hundred thousand people and one million animals fought for their lives. They were slaughtered for the enjoyment of this god and his friends.[5] The Latin word *arena* means "sand."[6] This arena, the Colosseum, was filled with sand to soak up all the blood. Too many victims were drowning in other people's blood, so someone devised this twisted solution to let the games continue. Just the idea of a god who would enjoy this cruelty and suffering is horrifying, but right from the beginning, God makes it very clear *that* is not who He is. God is the one who creates life, harmony, and all good things; and He tells us this is how He expects the world to operate.

God does not just create life; He *is* life. The ability to grow, reproduce, and have functional activity pours from Him. There was light before He formed the sun. From where did the light come? From Him. He made plants before He made the sun that grows the plants. How did the plants grow? From Him. He is light and life, and everything alive draws its life from Him. When anything alive loses its connection with Him, it loses its life source and begins the decaying process. Just as sunlight produces good-feeling chemicals in our brains and keeps our brains functioning, God produces life in our bodies, minds, souls, and relationships.

God also designed His creation to reproduce and give life to others. One of the tasks God gives man is to cultivate an environment that nurtures life. We are to give of ourselves to ensure others have life because we are made in His image to imitate Him. When He created life, light, harmony, beauty, and our ability to be life-giving beings, He said, "This is what I call *good!*"

Genesis 1 gives us lots of details and history, but most of

all, it tells us about a God who is worthy of worship. Everything we make has its roots in the first two chapters of Genesis. We cannot make any art with a color God did not create. We cannot make our favorite food without using His ingredients. We cannot even invent an imaginary creature without using the features of animals He already imagined. All our inspirations and creations are just remixes of what His mind has already conceived. The most valuable pieces of art we can create are simply echoes of what He has already imagined. He created everything we long for and value. No wonder He said it was *good*.

REFLECTION QUESTIONS:

This chapter tells us so much about who God is. What else did you notice about His character? What other contrasts can you make?

_____

_____

_____

_____

Take some time to stop and think. Imagine our God did not love the *good*. What if He enjoyed watching people and animals suffer? What would our physical environment look like? What would our relationships look like?

_____

_____

_____

_____

_____

Can you think of anything humans make that is not from
Genesis 1–2?

_____

_____

_____

_____

GENESIS 2

A nd the work was finished. All the pieces had come together perfectly. It was complete. Each animal was dependent on its habitat. Each habitat was designed to support that creature's life. God had created every environment and then filled each one with creatures uniquely made for it. Sea creatures were made to thrive in the water. Flying creatures were made to soar in the air. Land animals were made to inhabit the earth. Nothing was out of place. Nothing was lacking for the creation to flourish.

God enjoyed the completion of all the good He had created, so He rested, enjoying what He had made. Not only is God the one who created amazing wonders, but He is also the one who created rest and enjoyment. He knows when to work and when to rest. Although God created man in His own image and likeness, one of the biggest emotions humans struggle with is stress. We do not know how to get the rest we need to be rejuvenated, but we are created in the image of the one who does know and shows us how to do it.

God created Adam and gave him a name meaning "red dirt" in the Hebrew language. Adam is also the same word that will be used for humankind. When the Old Testament says *man*, it is actually calling us Adam. God has always been, but Adam or man has not always been. Life was not born into being. Rather, God created a grown man. Man was never alive until God breathed His life into Adam. God's Spirit is what brought man to life physically, socially, spiritually, and emotionally. As we read the account of God creating Adam, we cannot just view this as a far-off story that took place long ago. Whenever we say or think of the word *human*, we are supposed to remember Adam because we are all Adams. When God gives Adam his purpose, He is also giving us our purpose.

God gave Adam and his descendants the responsibility of managing God's beautiful world and blessed them. What does it mean that God blessed them? We don't go around "blessing" people these days. When God blessed Adam, He gave them His best. As a parent, my heart swells and overflows with the desire to give my children the best gifts. This desire actually comes from God, who created me in His image. I desire to give my children the best because God desires to give His children the best.[7]

If God wanted to give us the best and if He knew the consequences, why did He give us a choice? Let's list some other options God could have offered: He could have made us like robots so we would automatically do His will, or He could have locked us in a room with limited options where we would never be able to make a choice against Him. For there to be any genuine love, there must be freedom to make a choice. Just like a couple in a healthy marriage, God desires a relationship where we freely choose Him above all others. Since robots cannot have healthy relationships, there has to be an option to leave for us to choose to stay. God's gift of freedom was the *best* option.

God said, "Let Us make man in Our image." Again, we see

God is not a single Being. He created man in His image, which literally means His "statue."[8] God later forbids man from making statues of Him because He has already made statues of Himself. He made us. Anything created in the image of God *must* be living because *life* is an inherent part of who He is. After God created Adam, He couldn't say it was good or in harmony with who He is because man was alone. Life has never truly been lived until it selflessly gives itself away to another living being. God is making it clear that He exists in deep relationships, and this truth is key to what it means to be alive.

God chose to use a rib, which He had taken from Adam's side, in His creation of woman. We can see in creation there is nothing living that was not given life by another. God designed our purpose to give life and nurture life physically, socially, spiritually, and emotionally. We are to use the life God breathed into us to give life to others. When we do this, we truly come alive and find fulfillment. This aspect is a significant part of what it means to be made in the image of God.

REFLECTION QUESTIONS:

God created rest and knows how to do it well to bring completion to our own lives. How do you define rest? What does it mean for us to rest with God?

_____

_____

_____

_____

_____

Could God have created us with the ability to truly love Him without giving us free will?

_____

_____

_____

_____

_____

According to chapters 1 and 2, who was made in the image of God? Male or female? How does your answer affect your view of God?(After thinking through the question, read Genesis 1:27 again. Does this add any insight to your answer?)

_____

_____

_____

_____

_____

One of man's purposes was to nurture life. What does (or should) a nurturing life look like in your own life?

_____

_____

_____

_____

_____

GENESIS 3

H ere, we are introduced to the enemy of all goodness in the form of a serpent. The word *Satan* in Hebrew means "accuser/adversary."[9] God has just spent the last two pages telling us who He is and who we are. Now, this adversary pulls out his best trick against humanity. He does not lie to them, but he makes them question who God is and who they are. His first question is to ask them if God is really good or if God is less than who He says He is. The serpent's next question attacks the source of their self-worth, causing them to question if they are less than who God says they are. The serpent tempts them with promises that they will be more like God, even though they are already created in the image of God.

Satan also attacked Adam and Eve's relationship. Who did God tell not to eat the fruit? He told Adam before Eve was created, so Eve got her information from Adam. When Satan asked Eve,

"Did God really say …" he was not just making Eve question God; Satan was making Eve question Adam. God's image was not complete in man until man was living in a harmonious, giving relationship with another equal being. Satan throws a vicious wedge into their relationship with this simple question. Satan was trying to break man's relationship with God and man's relationship with man. He did this because he knew that anytime we break God's law, we also hurt our relationships with others.

Just as the enemy had promised, after Adam and Eve ate the fruit, they did see and know more. Suddenly, they knew fear; they could feel shame; they were able to experience pain. All of a sudden, their minds and hearts were opened to selfish, inward-focused desires. In that instant, they became the kind of beings who would give birth to sons who would kill one another and nations who would crave blood. Rather than responding with repentance, Adam and Eve each blamed someone else for their choices and the consequences. We, their children, also want to play the victim and blame others for our pain and poor choices. The moment Adam and Eve ate the fruit, we all became pain inflictors instead of life-givers.

What was perfect became broken. In His mercy, God took away the tree of life because He saw the evil they were capable of inflicting on one another. He couldn't allow them to inflict that pain for eternity. God knew that Adam and Eve needed restrictions to protect them from themselves. God knew that the new humans wouldn't value what didn't cost them. For them to value and protect life, there had to be pain when giving birth. They had become selfish, so there had to be a hierarchy to keep peace in the family and society. To keep man from multiplying evils, he needed to struggle to develop his character and occupy his time.

When Adam and Eve ate the fruit and rebelled against God, they rejected His definition of good and evil. Life can't be separated from goodness because both of those come from the essence of God. The moral code is connected with the genetic code. In the same way, death and evil can't be separated. Adam broke the moral code, and instantly, his cells began to die because he separated himself from the good. Because God's life-giving spirit had been rejected, Adam's imperishable body would fall apart until it became dirt again. Every newborn would be born with cells that were dying and a body that was slowly running out of life.

God's presence had brought peace, order, and all goodness. When man chose himself over the Life-Giver and Sustainer, the entire creation began to die and decay. Satan chose to hurt God by destroying His creation. How ironic that humans—created to represent the God of life, joy, and giving—would become creatures who built the Roman Colosseum and the Holocaust gas chambers and would create a child sex-trafficking empire. In doing these things, humankind was reflecting the deceiver rather than the life-giving God who created them.

We can't look at this story and blame Adam or Eve for their choices. This choice has become the story of every human. Adam and Eve decided they wanted to be the ones to determine what was good and evil, and we have been repeating their choices ever since. The next eight chapters tell us about human after human repeating this choice.

On this day, we walked away from God, but God didn't walk away from us. He killed an animal to cover Adam and Eve, showing that He was willing to sacrifice His creation to protect them. The skins that covered their nakedness were the couple's first experience of seeing death. Even at this point, they didn't comprehend everything they had lost, but Satan knew exactly what he had done to us. So God turned to the serpent and let him know that this wasn't over. God was not giving up on His creation. Here, we see our first glimpse of Jesus when God told Satan about one of Eve's descendants, "You will bruise His heel, but He will crush your head" (Genesis 3:15). The reckless love of God is on full display here as He tells Satan His intentions. God is saying even though the humans are walking away from him, he is not leaving them. He will do whatever it takes to bring them life again.

REFLECTION QUESTIONS:

Satan uses these same tricks on us that he used on Eve: (1) he leads us to a skewed view of God, and (2) he leads us to a skewed view of ourselves. How have you seen Satan use these tactics in your own life? What lies do you hear Satan tell you about who God is and who you are? How does he challenge you to doubt God?

_____

_____

_____

_____

Think of a time you did something wrong. Were you tempted to make an excuse for your actions? Did your excuse put the blame on someone or something else? Why do we struggle to take responsibility for our choices?

_____

_____

_____

_____

_____

GENESIS 4

What was so wrong with eating some fruit? Oftentimes, we get caught up in that detail and miss what really happened to Adam and Eve. Keep in mind it was not just one choice they made but a series of choices *without repentance*. They chose to doubt God. They chose to be discontent. They chose to disobey and take the fruit. They chose to hide. They chose to turn against each other. They wouldn't humble themselves and ask for forgiveness. They chose to walk away. God had designed them to be the caretakers and nurturers of life, but they wanted all life to serve them. They were completely different people with different hearts. We have no biblical evidence that they ever asked God to forgive them or to restore what was broken. God had to limit their power to keep them from abusing other lives to fulfill their own selfish desires.

The consequences of this heart change were a break in the

relationship with God and a break in the relationship with each other. Every time someone sins, it hurts not only their relationship with God but also their relationships with other people. The seed that Adam and Eve planted now blossoms and bears its devastating fruit.

We begin to see what this broken relationship looks like right away between two of Adam and Eve's sons. Abel gave a gift to God from the best he had. God was pleased with it. Cain gave a gift to God that wasn't his best. God wasn't pleased. God told Cain if he would offer God his best, God would be pleased, but Cain chose himself over God as his parents had. God warned Cain that he had free will. God told him what the consequences would be if he chose to determine good and evil for himself. Cain "took the fruit" and did what was right in his own eyes. After Cain killed his brother, God asked him what he had done. He repeated his parents' choice when he made it clear to God that he was only concerned for himself. God told Cain there was still a standard, so there must be justice. However, God, in His mercy, won't allow this sinful choice to be the end of Cain. He still tried to protect Cain from himself. Humankind has gone from being nurturers of life to being takers of life.

Cain left and started a city where his descendants began defining good and evil for themselves. One of Cain's descendants, Lamech, sang a song bragging about how he was much more violent and murderous than Cain. This song also tells us that Lamech took more than one wife. Why does the Bible put this awful man in the story? The Bible is not a story about good *people* but about a *God who is faithful to unfaithful people.*

Notice that this is the first time in the Bible that we see a man having more than one wife. The Bible uses this point as evidence that Lamech was a wicked man because having multiple partners was *not* God's plan for marriage. God's plan was that each partner would be equal in value with different strengths and solely devoted to the well-being of the other. Each marriage was supposed to consist of one woman and one man who belonged only to each other. Here, Lamech decided he wanted to have more than one other person who belonged completely to him, but he didn't completely belong to either of them. This account is where we start to see men devaluing women and taking women as possessions. Notice as we see men collecting women that it *always* causes problems.

We have now experienced some of the pain and death that God told Adam and Eve about in the last chapter. Why did God allow pain? Pain is actually not the real problem; death and destruction are the problem. Once death was introduced into our world, God gave us the gift of pain. Without pain, we see no need to avoid things that hurt or kill us. Pain is what makes us pull back our hands when we touch fire so that our hand is not consumed. The pain of imprisonment keeps some people from killing others. The pain of loneliness pushes us to mend broken relationships. After Eden, we are no longer motivated by goodness, so now we have to be motivated by fear and pain. Pain is a gift that protects us from ourselves and protects others from the harm we are capable of inflicting.

Adam and Eve walked away from God because they had no fear or concern for the death that would come. They didn't even bother to turn around and ask God to teach them how to live in this broken world. This chapter tells us some of the consequences that followed Adam and Eve's choices and ends with humanity calling out to God for deliverance from themselves. The pain they endured told them they needed God to avoid the death that they were consuming and that was consuming them.

REFLECTION QUESTION

Something was lacking in Cain's gift because it wasn't Cain's best. What motivates us to hold back the best for ourselves instead of giving God the best?

_____

_____

_____

_____

_____

I've heard people say that pornography doesn't hurt anyone else, but the models used in pornography have one of the highest self-harm and suicide rates.[10] Can you think of a sin we commit that doesn't hurt another human? If not, what consequences does it have?

_____

_____

_____

_____

If we were left to define good and evil by ourselves and didn't have pain, shame, or fear, how would people behave? Without these consequences, what would stop you or society from hurting others? If we didn't have to work for our needs, what would we spend all day doing?

_____

GENESIS 5

At the end of the last chapter, man, or Adam, began calling on the Lord; and here, God is reminding man that man was created to reflect His image and character. After reading chapter 4 about Lamech using women like property and boasting about his murderous heart, we need to be reminded that this is not how man was supposed to live. God reminds us that He gave us the best of everything right from the beginning.

Adam was created in God's image to dwell in God's presence in a place where heaven and earth overlapped. When humanity turned its back on God, we chose to live without God's presence. Six generations in the line of Seth and nearly five hundred years later, we are introduced to the first image bearer mentioned, who sought to dwell in God's presence. Heaven and earth overlapped once more in God's relationship with Enoch. Why did God choose Enoch? The Bible never says that God chose Enoch but that Enoch chose God.

God's initial plan was for Adam and Eve to walk with Him in the garden, but they walked away instead. Most of Adam and Eve's descendants followed in their footsteps and also walked away from God, but Enoch made the choice to walk with God. Enoch's brief testimony is a reminder of God's character that God had not walked away from humanity. He was just waiting for someone to choose Him. Death is the result of the absence of the Life-Giver and sustainer. Enoch walked in the presence of the God of life, and he was the first human who didn't experience physical death. What does that mean for people who desire to walk with God? It means our companion is powerful and unpredictable.

Throughout this genealogy of eleven generations of men made in the image of God, Enoch is the first one whose character is mentioned to reflect God's. The genealogy starts with Adam and ends with Noah's sons. Check out how long these guys were living! Why did God shorten people's lives after this time? As a mental health counselor, I (Ruth) once heard that people become more of who they are the older they get.[11] Since then, I have seen this play out over and over. Kind people become kinder. Critical people become more critical. Selfish people become more selfish. The limits of evil are only constrained by our imagination. The more time people have, the more evil they can conceive. The more evil they conceive, the more pain they inflict. Keep this in mind as you read the next chapter!

The chapter ends with Lamech naming his son. This individual is not the same Lamech from the previous chapter. This man is Seth's descendant, not Cain's. Lamech is mourning the evil, death, and destruction that they are enduring; and he hopes that Noah will bring peace and life to the world. Here, the chapter ends and leaves us hanging.

Many people think that the Bible is an account of God creating heaven and hell. Good people go to heaven, and bad people go to hell,[12] but this is not the story of the Bible. Genesis 1 clearly states that God created heaven and earth. Heaven is the place where God lives, and the Earth is the place where man lives. We often assume these places are completely separate, but the story of the Bible is all about how God is trying to unite heaven and earth. God created heaven and earth to be united in the garden.[13]

His whole kingdom is built on the principles of goodness and life from the genetic makeup to the moral code, but once we decided to define right and wrong ourselves, everything in us was fighting against that environment. Paradise was no longer comfortable because we were no longer good. It was a place where we felt ashamed, covered ourselves, and hid because our hearts no longer belonged there. Heaven left the place where the humans lived, but God never stopped His mission of uniting our home with His. This plan will continue to unfold throughout the story of the Bible. One day, He is going to breathe His life-giving Spirit back into man just like He did in the garden so that our hearts also desire to be life-givers. After this radical heart change, we can be at home in His presence, and He will unite heaven and earth once again.

REFLECTION QUESTIONS:

Who can walk with God? What does it mean to walk with God?

_____

_____

_____

_____

_____

Verse 3 says that Seth was made in Adam's image, so even though he was made in God's image, he has now inherited Adam's brokenness. What does this mean for you and me?

_____

_____

_____

_____

Does it change your view of God when you realize that God originally created heaven and earth, not heaven and hell, as part of His good creation?

_____

_____

_____

_____

_____

GENESIS 6

Who were these "sons of God"? The Bible doesn't make it clear who these mighty men were. Some think these could be evil angels; others think they could be descendants of Seth's God-fearing line who intermarried with unbelievers.[14] Whoever this group of people may be, they are not serving God and are definitely not reflecting the character of the Life-Giver. Like Lamech, they collected wives like cattle for their own pleasure. They had children who were mighty warriors trained to destroy life. God saw that they were constantly daydreaming of how much pain and destruction they could inflict on others. He was heartbroken for everyone and everything He created. Only one man found favor in His sight.

The third verse directs our attention back to the character of God. God made it clear that the way they were treating their women and the violence they were committing against others was in complete opposition to everything He is. He declared that He wouldn't let humans continue to inflict this kind of pain and injustice for long. Then, He set a limit: 120 years and they were done. The 120 years could be referring to the length of time until the upcoming flood, or it could mean God was shortening man's lifespan to about 120 years. It could mean both.[15] The main point is that God is still the Life-Giver, and humans are still held accountable for the pain they inflict and the life they take. God was letting them know that He took no pleasure in the pain that He was about to unleash on the world, but for the good of creation and man's redemption, He must limit the power of the wicked.

God decided the best course of action was to start over with Noah, his family, and a selection of animals. God told us that Noah had chosen to live by God's definition of good and evil and walk with Him. He knew that the rest of the humans living on the earth were life-takers and destroyers. No one was innocent. God then gave very specific instructions to Noah about how to build the ark, what to have on it, and how to plan. Genesis 2:6 says that God watered the earth with a mist that came up from the ground. The mention of rain here in chapter 6 is the first in the book, so it is possible that rain and flooding were foreign concepts for everyone. Despite how bizarre this sounded, Noah did *all* that God told him to do. Here, we see the contrast between the first humans and Noah. Noah didn't dwell on his doubts. He didn't allow himself to become discontent. Instead, Noah did exactly as God commanded, even though it didn't make sense. He took responsibility for himself and others and chose to dwell in the presence of the Life-Giver.

REFLECTION QUESTIONS:

God's call on Noah's life seemed fanatical to everyone around him. Why doesn't God call people to do radical things like that today? Or does He?

_____

_____

_____

_____

_____

Why were all the animals (besides the ones on the ark) punished because of man?

_____

_____

_____

_____

How does our sin today affect the rest of creation, including the animals and our environment?

_____

_____

_____

_____

GENESIS 7

We start this chapter with God giving directions to Noah about when and how to start this voyage. God reiterated His reasoning behind His decision. Humans were destroying everything, including themselves and one another. Noah was the only one who hadn't "taken the fruit" to determine good and evil for himself. It doesn't tell us whether or not Noah's sons were representing God's character along with Noah; it just says that God chose the three sons—Shem, Ham, and Japheth—to help Noah rebuild this world.

Here, we see our first glimpse of clean versus unclean animals. What is that all about? God doesn't explain much in this passage, but God is giving them this distinction as a reminder. The broken earth was now operating on a system of humans using and consuming other lives, which is the complete opposite of heaven's system, where we are made in God's image to give and nurture life. Clean versus unclean animals was a symbol to remind them that they were made for heaven's system.[16] He was telling them they were to give of themselves sacrificially, but they couldn't do this until they had been transformed by God into beings that are "clean." This whole sacrificial and dietary system would become an example for all of Noah's descendants to follow. It would remind them of heaven's reality and their true purpose.

Why did God gather all these animals and save them on the ark? Why didn't God just create new animals once the people had been saved? God was displaying His character once again in this act. Even though humans had really made a mess of His good world, He was committed to them and life's sustenance. He was not giving up His plan to unite heaven and earth once again. The flood that God released gives us the idea of the earth reverting to its former state of being: a dark wasteland covered by deep waters. By the end of the chapter, every creature on the earth that breathed God's life-giving spirit was floating on a boat, being sustained by the Life-Giver and waiting to start again.

So what happened to all the people killed in the flood? Did God send them to hell? Earlier, we discussed that in the beginning, God created heaven and earth. Heaven was the place where God lived and where life, beauty, justice, and goodness reigned. Earth was the place where man lived, and God's original plan was that heaven and earth would be united; but then, man brought sin, ugliness, oppression, and death to the earth. Heaven and earth had to separate because they couldn't coexist.

Whatever hell is, there is no place in Genesis that says it was created by God with the intention of punishing humans.[17] James 3 tells us that when humans use their tongues to tear one another down, we are "lit on fire by hell." So hell is not only a reality in the future but also a reality now. Hell is something that is lit and grown within ourselves and then inflicted on others.[18] The hell in our hearts has created a child sex-trafficking ring that consists of about a million children worldwide. It birthed a Rwandan genocide in 1994, where eight hundred thousand people were slaughtered in one hundred days.[19] The hell in our hearts is responsible for every evil thought and every evil deed. It is everything that God is not, and God hates it, but we grow it in our hearts. The story of the Bible is about God's desire to get rid of the hell in our world so that He can unite heaven and earth again. To take the hell out of this world, He has to either take the hell out of us or take us out of this world.[20]

So let's answer the question, "Did God send them to hell?" C. S. Lewis in *The Dark Tower* reminds us that "a man can't be taken to hell, or sent to hell: you can only get there on your own stream."[21] From the moment the first Adam took the fruit, heaven was no longer where we felt at home. Hell began burning and growing in our very souls. Every evil thought and every evil deed flamed this fire that was kindled in our hearts. The story of each human life can be summed up with us telling God either "Thy will be done" or "My will be done."[22] God gives us the choice. The only way God can take the hell out of us is by surrendering to His will and allowing His power to transform us to the core. This process is painful but wonderful. Part of us dies, but it is the part that was killing us anyway!

REFLECTION QUESTIONS:

The destruction and devastation caused by the flood were truly catastrophic! Wouldn't it have been easier just to send a plague or zap them with an angel or something? Why do you think God chose this method to deal with man's sinfulness?

_____

_____

_____

_____

_____

The evilness of man had become so great that God, for a moment, regretted ever making man! What do God's regret and God's response reveal about His character? What does His provision for Noah, his family, and the creatures reveal about His character?

_____

_____

_____

_____

_____

GENESIS 8

This chapter begins by echoing the creation narrative. In the first chapter of Genesis, the Holy Spirit was hovering over the waters. The Hebrew word for *spirit* there is *ruach*. After the flood, God sent a wind to pass over the waters on the earth. Guess what He called the wind? It is the same Hebrew word: *ruach*. Coincidence? I think not. This account is setting us up for a new beginning. The flood had destroyed the wickedness of the land like no other method could have. The satanic temples were gone, the idols were gone, and the wicked literature that glorified violence and oppression was gone. The culture was ready to be rewritten on a clean slate. Would Noah and his family walk with God and help to reunite heaven and earth?

The flood account was no small event. From the time Noah entered the ark until Noah and his companions stepped onto the dry land, 377 days (just over a year) had passed. This chapter provides a lot of details about the voyage, the earth's conditions, and Noah's responses.

After Noah sets foot on dry ground, this chapter includes a somewhat disturbing scene from our modern perspective. Noah offered God a sacrifice of burning animals, and God said that He enjoyed the aroma. What kind of being would enjoy the smell of death? What is *that* all about?

Back in the garden, after Adam and Eve realized there was something wrong with them, God killed an animal to clothe and protect them. Time and time again, throughout the last few chapters, God has made it clear that He is willing to prioritize His relationship with humanity over His protection of His good creation. This act is one way He shows us the seriousness of the hell in our hearts. David echoed this truth in Psalm 51:16–17 (NKJV), "For You do not desire sacrifice, or else I would give it; You do not delight in burnt offering. The sacrifices of God are a broken spirit, a broken and a contrite heart—These, O God, You will not despise." Similarly, when God was speaking to an unrepentant people going through religious motions, Isaiah wrote, "'To what purpose is the multitude of your sacrifices to Me?' Says the Lord. 'I have had enough of burnt offerings of rams and the fat of fed cattle. I do not delight in the blood of bulls, or of lambs or goats'" (Isaiah 11:1 NKJV).[23]

If God doesn't like the sacrifice itself, why did He want them to do it? The sacrifice is actually for the sake of *man*. The animal is slaughtered; and as its life drains away, the scene is an ugly, bloody, and gross depiction of how the hell in man's hearts is destroying not only them but also all the good life God created. The point is for the person who committed the sin to become sickened at the gory sight and smell. Hopefully, this will help them realize this death is what is happening to them and everything they touch. Since hell entered our thoughts, we have been bleeding to death emotionally, physically, spiritually, and relationally with one another. We just don't realize the seriousness of what is happening to us because we have grown accustomed to dying. The sight is meant to humble us to ask God to breathe His life-giving Spirit back into our hearts again.

After Eden, many times in the Old Testament, when God meets with people, He asks them to create a clean space for Him to come. Death and sin have infected the entire creation, including us. Somehow, the death of innocent animals and the humility it takes to do this create a space that is holy for God to come and meet with His people. God tells Moses later on that God couldn't meet face-to-face with him because God's presence would be too much, and Moses wouldn't survive. When we boil water, the heat purifies the water by killing the germs. The entire creation, including us, is filled with the germs of sin that can't live in the presence of God. Being in God's presence would be deadly to us, but it seems the animal absorbs the "heat" that purifies so we can be in God's presence. One day, Jesus would come and absorb all the heat so we could be purified, and God could breathe his Holy Spirit into us again. Once again, God shows us that He is willing to use His creation to protect humans.

The point of the sacrifice is also for us to realize that all the hell we create must be judged and atoned for. A substitute that is "clean" of our disease has to take our death if we are to have life again. Let's be honest, an animal can't fix our sin problem. As the Old Testament sacrificial system continues to unfold, we'll begin to see how it is a "foreshadowing" of God's ultimate redemption plan in the perfect God-Man, Jesus. For the time being, this is the closest imagery these people have to Jesus. We *should* think this animal sacrifice is appalling and painful so that it can lead us to see the hell in our hearts for how ugly it really is. It should lead us to see our need for redemption. It is also God's promise that a clean and pure being will come and take our death so we can choose life. It wasn't the death that God was pleased with; it was the fact that Noah was humbling himself by choosing to accept God's definition of good and evil. He was asking God to take the hell out of his heart and unite heaven and earth once again.

The end of the chapter wraps up with God making a promise that He will do what He can to help man succeed in cultivating the land to produce and nourish life. God makes an interesting promise that as long as the earth exists, He will balance seasons, the weather, and the days so that the entire earth will never be under the same devastating weather conditions again.

REFLECTION QUESTIONS:

If God had not destroyed the environment that the humans had created (the idols, the satanic temples, etc.) along with the wicked people, how do you think that would have affected Noah's children?

_____

_____

_____

_____

_____

God has shown us that He is willing to prioritize His relationship with humanity over His good creation as a means to show us the seriousness of the hell in our hearts. What does this say about what He thinks about who you are? What does this say about the type of relationship He wants with you?

_____

_____

_____

_____

_____

GENESIS 9

This chapter begins on a positive note. God gave man another chance. This chapter mirrors what we read in Genesis 1–2. God had made the world clean of the evil that humans had created, and He told them to start again. God's command began similar to those given to Adam in Eden by God. God gave humans His blessing, and He gave them a similar job to what He gave to Adam. He commanded them to go and nurture a world where life can flourish. They are to be little life-givers reflecting His image.

However, God gave them some expectations that were going to be different from the ones He gave in Eden. Note that God didn't tell them that they still have dominion over the world and the animal kingdom. When man's relationship with God changed in the garden, man's relationship with the world and the animals changed as well. In the garden, man was supposed to nurture life. Man's heart had changed; as a result, he was now capable of all types of cruelty. Changing man's role with the animals was necessary to keep man from abusing the world and the animals for his own pleasure.

Many studies show that humans who enjoy cruelty to animals also enjoy cruelty to other humans.[24] God provided these new commands to help them establish a sense of respect for the animals and even more so for other humans. In Eden, there was no fear because there was no death. Since humans still have the ability to create hell in their hearts, heaven has not reunited with earth yet. Therefore, there is still death. To protect both man and animals from each other, God instilled an inherent fear of humans in every animal that He has created.

God also gave new humanity some rules by which to live. He told them that they were free to eat any animal or plant, but they were not to eat anything that was still living. He defines *living as* anything that still has blood flowing in its body. This directive is our first glimpse of the symbolism of blood that God will continue to use throughout the rest of the biblical story. The emphasis on the sacredness of the lifeblood will help to ensure that animals are not killed needlessly but in such a way that will minimize pain and cruelty. While man is permitted to kill animals for food, humans are *not* permitted to kill one another. God was making a clear distinction between the value of human life and the value of animal life. God established serious consequences for any man or creature who killed one of His image bearers. Earlier, God had not required Cain to die for killing Abel; but now, anyone who intentionally murders another human is also to be killed.

Next, we see the covenant between God and Noah. Until this point, we have not seen anything like this. A covenant is often compared to a promise or a contract, but it is actually so much more.[25] A contract is built on distrust of the other party and then considered obsolete if the other party breaks it. A contract assumes that the ones entering it are untrustworthy, but a covenant is built on a trusting relationship between two parties and was often intended to last generations. If one party breaks the covenant, the other party is still bound to it. A covenant went beyond death and was to be fulfilled by the descendants. This covenant that God initiated with Noah was based solely on God's character. No matter what humans may do, He will fulfill His promise.[26] So when God made this covenant, He was also making this promise with every human who descended from Noah.

Whenever God initiates a covenant with man, God makes promises and often asks man to make commitments in return. There are four times in the Old Testament that God initiates covenants with humans, and they are all for the purpose of blessing all of humanity, not just the individual. God's promise to Noah was that even though He knew humans were going to keep growing hell in their hearts, He wouldn't destroy the earth with a flood again. The rainbow that often appears after a rainstorm is a reminder to both us and God that He will never again interfere with the earth's weather patterns to destroy all of humanity. This covenant is different from the other covenants that God initiates because the other three covenants ask for a commitment from man, but this one doesn't.[27] God is saying that He knows they will eat the fruit again and continue to inflict hell on others, but He promises to be faithful in pursuing them.

So things were off to a great start until Noah literally ate the fruit. Similar to Eden, Noah was in a garden, but he got smashed. Once he was really drunk, his son Ham did something shameful to him in Noah's tent. The Bible doesn't give us the details, but it tells us all we need to know. Now, the second Adam is also naked and ashamed and has also failed, but God already knew man's heart, and He promised to be faithful anyway.

REFLECTION QUESTIONS:

As humanity is getting a new start, what does this chapter reveal about the character of God?

_____

_____

_____

_____

_____

If we view life and the blood of both man and animals as sacred, how does that affect the way we treat the animal kingdom? How does that affect the way we treat other humans?

_____

_____

_____

_____

_____

Are you one of Noah's descendants? If so, how does God's covenant with Noah apply to you today?

_____

_____

_____

_____

_____

GENESIS 10

Welcome to the Bible's Ancestry.com. In the last chapter, God told Noah to be fruitful and multiply and fill the earth. Here, we have the fulfillment of that command in this "table of nations" chapter. God loves diversity. He created diversity. He desired that Noah's children would spread out and establish their own families and cultures. However, as we'll see in the next chapter, God had to intervene to make this happen. The nations listed here become key figures in the biblical story.

While the list isn't comprehensive, and many of these people groups have been lost to history, we see Shem's kids heading off in the direction of the Middle East. The family of Abraham and the Israelites will come from this branch of the family tree. Japheth's kids head northward, likely to settle in the northern Mediterranean area and Europe. Ham's kids will lead to nations around Palestine and North Africa. Over the course of the next four thousand years, people groups continue to expand and overlap. This genealogy also reminds us that regardless of our ethnic background today, we are all part of *one* family with equal value.

Why do we have this long list of families? We are getting ready to deal with many of these nations in the next few chapters. This list provides lots of perspective on where these families came from and how they got there. One reason that this list is provided here is that it makes connections for us.

We just finished the story of God blessing Noah's family, and then Noah's son Ham was cursed for his immoral actions toward his dad. Children tend to follow the example of their parents, and this chapter tells us who Ham's children became. We soon find out that they quickly became even more wicked than his siblings' descendants. God would later use the children of Israel to curb the wicked appetites and practices of Ham's kids. The Canaanites were the people the Israelites would attempt to drive out of the Promised Land many generations later. This chapter helps us see who did what, how each family developed, and then how God responded.

Halfway through this genealogy, we are introduced to a man named Nimrod, another of Ham's descendants. He was said to be "a mighty hunter before the Lord." As we looked at the original text, the phrase doesn't suggest that he walked with God but rather that he was famous for his skill and violence against the Lord and that God was very much aware of this man's influence.[28] This man and his kids went on to establish the cities of Nineveh, Assyria, and Babel or Babylon. These cities soon became famous for their violence and torture and later, in the biblical story, became chief enemies of Israel.

Verse 13 includes another of Ham's sons named Mizraim; this man was the father of the nation of Egypt. It is baffling to think about how one of Ham's descendants would start a family who would enslave some of Shem's descendants (the Israelites) for four hundred years. Talk about a dysfunctional family!

This chapter isn't just giving us a chronology, but it is getting us mentally and emotionally prepared for a long journey. God's journey with man is heartbreaking as He watches generation after generation eating the fruit. We are reaching for pleasure with all our strength while standing on the bodies of others just to get a little closer. While striving to live our lives to the fullest, we don't realize that we are actually the animal that is bleeding to death. Running around with the motto "You only live once," we excuse our selfish actions and thoughts. We think our pornography, degrading thoughts of others, and secret sins aren't hurting anyone as we create a hell that eats us alive. The Life-Giver is pursuing us as we pursue ourselves. He has made a covenant that He won't give up on us.

REFLECTION QUESTIONS:

When you think about the human race as one family, does it change the way you think about other ethnic groups?

_____

_____

_____

_____

If you truly saw your neighbors, coworkers, and passing strangers as cousins, how might that affect the way you treat them? What are some things you could do to help bring unity and healing to our one human family?

_____

_____

_____

_____

_____

What are some ways that even "good people" hurt others? What can the Life-Giver do in your relationships with others?

_____

_____

_____

_____

_____

GENESIS 11

W e just finished the "table of nations" chapter, which can be overwhelming. Now, we take a step back—actually, a couple of steps back—to Noah and his children. What was the whole point of the flood? Noah's family saw firsthand how evil humans became when they didn't follow God's law of good and evil. Now, Noah's family was to spread out on the earth and do what Adam and Eve failed to do. They were to be life-givers and nurturers by trusting God's definition of good and evil.

So chapter 11 begins with Noah's kids and their families all huddled together, living their lives. They all had the same cultural background, spoke the same language, and had similar life goals. God had told them in chapter 9 to spread throughout the earth, but they didn't want to. Why did it matter if they wanted to stick together? Their motive for sticking together wasn't to help one another but to help themselves. The people did what was convenient, not what was commanded. Their culture glorified self-gratification and self-glorification. They wanted to build a strong city so that they could determine good and evil for themselves without anyone stopping them. They were eating the fruit again but with the "strength in numbers" idea. While there is nothing inherently wrong with building a city or a tower, the tower they built, the Tower of Babel, became a way to prop up their arrogance and pride in security. Of course, there was no real security in bricks, but the false sense of security would allow them to create hell in their hearts without fear of the ramifications. They needed the fear of the Lord to keep them from destroying themselves and others. This tower was an attempt to prove they were powerful like God.[29]

They were so proud of how smart and self-sufficient they were and felt that they did not need the Life Sustainer. They determined that they would make a name for themselves so that all people would know who they were. The ironic thing is that God did make a famous name for them! Here we are, four thousand years later, having a conversation about these babbling people. The word Babel in Hebrew actually means "confusion,"[30] so these people have been known for several millennia as those poor, confused people. The name Babel is the same word in the Hebrew language for Babylon. The city of Babylon is mentioned about 250 times in the Hebrew Bible, becoming a representation of the human race. Whenever Babylon is mentioned in the Bible, the author is telling us that we already know where the story is going. Babylon is a symbol showing us that Adam, or humanity, always ends up as slaves to wickedness when we determine right and wrong for ourselves.[31]

Was God afraid that they would succeed if He didn't stop them? Um, no. While they wanted to build the tower "to reach heaven," God knew the snake was speaking to them with his garden song, saying, "You can be like God." God's not as concerned about their technological or architectural achievement as He is with their limitless lust for evil. God knew if they banded together, there would be no limit to the evil their hearts would imagine. The world wars are enough evidence that God was right.

Can you think of a more painless way to disband a group of selfish people? No fight or violence was recorded, no famine or plague; the confused people just moved on. When we don't understand God's ways, we have to trust He is the Life-Giver, and He is good. We should also note that God is the author of the world's language families. Anything God creates is good. While the circumstances surrounding the birth of the world languages are saddening, we can celebrate the diversity of creation.

This chapter ends with a shift from a global perspective to a narrowing focus on one family: a line from Shem to Abram. This genealogy is preparing us for not only the next chapter but also the rest of the Old Testament story as it hones in on God's journey with this dysfunctional big family to bring about the redemption of humanity. God has not forgotten His words to the snake. Another Adam would be coming, who would take the place of the first Adam. The snake would bite His heel, but the second Adam would crush his head. When we look back at the New Testament, we can see that God is giving us the genealogy from Eve to Jesus just so we know it wasn't an accident. This second Adam was His plan from the very beginning with His first words to the snake. One way to sum up these first eleven chapters would be that the human race keeps eating the deadly fruit, and we aren't going to stop without an outside intervention.

REFLECTION QUESTIONS:

The residents of Babel prided themselves in the security of their unified language and fortified city, which led them to think they knew better than God. What securities or comforts do we tend to cling to that may interfere with God's calling on our lives?

_____

_____

_____

_____

_____

The people of Babel were proud of their latest and greatest technology: the brick. While this may sound silly to us, how does our own technology make us feel superior today?

_____

_____

_____

_____

While there was nothing wrong with building a tower or living in a city, the motive behind these choices was wrong. What personal examples can you think of that aren't necessarily wrong in and of themselves but could be bad if done with wrong motives?

_____

_____

_____

_____

GENESIS 12

N ow, the story takes a big turn. We go from the history of the world over thousands of years to zooming in on one family. We immediately think, "Why is this family so special? Why did God choose to bless them?" As we continue to read, we realize this family is not a group of really amazing people; in fact, they were a seriously dysfunctional family! But this story isn't about them. This story is about the Life-Giver who is committed to pursuing all of us, and He chooses to use this family to bring about a blessing to all of humanity.

This chapter begins with a poem of God telling Abram to go to an unknown destination. Then God blessed him, saying that God would give him numerous descendants, make him prosper, make him famous, and fight his battles for him. God basically promised Abram that he would become King Abram if He would follow God in faith and obedience. Keep in mind that Abram was a seventy-five-year-old man living with his parents and had no children. Abram's response, "Yes, please!"

If I were God, looking for someone to represent me, I wouldn't choose this guy. I would choose someone who looks like they have their life together at least a little. With the calling of Abram, we begin to notice a theme: God often picks people who seem unlikely candidates but are *willing* to follow Him. God made it clear that the reason He did this was so that everyone else on the earth would be blessed through Abram's family. He didn't do this because He loved Abram more than the others. He did this because He loves all people. God wanted someone who would show the rest of the people what the Life-Giver can do when humans choose to accept His definition of good and evil.

Abram set off with everything he had, along with his nephew Lot. The previous chapter mentioned Lot's father dying young, so it looks like Abram took over that fatherly role in Lot's life. They began to wander wherever God led them until God paused and told Abram that his descendants would occupy this land right here. Immediately, Abram stopped and built an altar to God. Remember, the altar and sacrifice were a way for humans to humble themselves, admit they need the Life-Giver, and accept God's standard of good and evil. Abram was unusual. Abram didn't just do this once; he built an altar and sacrificed twice. This attitude is a level of humility we haven't seen in previous characters in the story so far.

So God led Abram to a new Promised Land, but then, Abram almost immediately left it! Rather than trusting God to provide, Abram and his people sought security in Egypt. Because the Nile River flowed through it, the land of Egypt had the advantage of a steady water supply and fertile soil surrounding the river. When they arrived, Abram told his wife, Sarai, to play along as he passed her off as his sister. Technically, Abram was telling the truth. Sarai was Abram's half sister, but she was also his wife. Abram intentionally sought to deceive the Egyptian leaders because he knew she was beautiful, and the leaders in Egypt would want to have her as their own. As her brother and protector, not only would his life be spared, but they would also treat him as an honored guest. At this moment, Abram was willing to trade his wife for food as though she was his property.

God made it clear in Eden when He created woman that both she and the man are a part of the living "statue" that represents Him. Both are equally deserving of dignity and respect. The relationship between the man and the woman is to be life-giving and protecting. Not only are the individuals both representatives of God's character, but their relationship is also part of what makes them His image bearers. Abram blew this big time, resulting in personal embarrassment and shame. Later, we will see the ramifications of family dysfunction that spiraled out of this move.

One of the Egyptian officials took Sarai to become one of his wives and gave Abram lots of goodies in the trade. Selling relationships for stuff was Abram's definition of "good," but it is God's definition of evil. God communicated to the Egyptians by doing what the Egyptians would expect one of their gods to do when they were displeased. God spoke the Egyptians' language. Then, Pharaoh publicly denounced Abram's character and told him to leave. The ironic thing is that Abram was supposed to be showing them who God is by reflecting God through his actions, but instead, the Egyptians seem to be more moral in this story than Abram. Abram was sent away with the reputation of being an immoral scoundrel and cheat.

Here, Eden repeats itself once again. God had already promised Abram that he would be given the best, prosper, have lots of descendants, and obviously live longer because he had no descendants yet. God had promised that anyone who blessed Abram, God would bless. Anyone who cursed Abram, God would curse. The snake was once again asking Abram, "Is God really who He says He is? Are you really who He says you are?" In response, Abram doubted God's character, provisions, and protection. He desired to prosper his own way. He was turning his back on his wife to take care of himself, and he was kicked out of the garden of Egypt by other humans for not representing the character of God. Abram was no hero, but God is. God followed Abram as he crawled out of Egypt, and then God patiently taught Abram *how* to follow the Life-Giver.

REFLECTION QUESTIONS:

God called Abram out of his homeland and away from his family to an unknown destination. How has God called you out of your comfort zone to follow Him?

_____

_____

_____

_____

Some think that God might have originally called Terah to follow Him to Canaan, but he got distracted along the way.[32] Similarly, Abram quickly left the land God promised to him when times got difficult. How are you tempted through distraction from what He has called you to do?

_____

_____

_____

_____

_____

What was Abram so afraid of in Egypt that he was willing to give up his wife? Think about all the things God had already promised Abram. Was there anything Abram was afraid of that God had not already promised? How has the devil tempted you recently to doubt who God is and who He says you are?

_____

_____

_____

_____

_____

Why did God stick with Abram after he blew it so early in their relationship together? What does this say about God?

_____

_____

_____

_____

_____

GENESIS 13

fter his humiliating experience, Abram and his people left the fertile garden land of Egypt to hang out in the Negev (your Bible may simply say the South). The Negev is a largely hot, barren desert with very little rain. It was here in the desert that Abram's possessions and riches seemed to multiply. Whoa, wait a minute. Abraham went to Egypt because he lacked faith that God would provide for him in difficult times. Then, in a barren region, God prospered Abram, and he became very wealthy. God demonstrated that He would provide for His people even in challenging circumstances. Now, if only we could learn to wait on Him.

After this season in the Negev, Abram returned the way he had come earlier to Canaan and ended up in the same place where he had first built an altar to God. This place was sacred to Abram because he had met with God there. Abram again called out to

God and sought to realign himself with the character of God by asking God to define what is good and evil for Abram.

Just as God had been blessing Abram, Abram's nephew Lot, who had been traveling with Abram, was getting wealthy too. Remember God's promise to Abram earlier? As God blessed Abram, He also blessed others who joined Abram. Soon, Abram and Lot had so much stuff and so many animals that the land wasn't big enough to support them both. They decided to split up. Although God promised the land to Abram, Abram was generous and told Lot to pick first. Lot picked the most fertile land, which also happened to be near the rich and wicked city of Sodom. Lot set up camp just outside this wicked city. Here, we begin to see some key differences in Abram's and Lot's choices. Lot takes the easy path where the riches and comforts are, but Abram begins to rely on God.

After Lot's departure, God reiterated His promise and blessing to Abram. God asked Abram to look around and focus on all he had instead of what he didn't have. He was asking Abram to trust Him that He would give Abram what was truly good instead of what looked good in the big city. Once again, Abram's response was to build another altar to the Lord, this time in Hebron. Abram was humbling himself and surrendering to God. Abram refused to eat the fruit of discontentment and doubt in God. Abram was choosing to believe that God is who He says He is and that Abram is who God says he is.

REFLECTION QUESTIONS:

In what areas does Satan try to make us discontent? How does God's provision and blessing of Abram in the Negev help you trust Him?

_____

_____

_____

_____

_____

What do you think Lot found attractive about the city? How would living in this region make life easier? What are some similar temptations we have today that can call us away from God's plan for our lives?

_____

_____

_____

_____

Our attitude is a choice that helps determine our actions. What kinds of attitudes did Abram choose in this chapter?

_____

_____

_____

_____

GENESIS 14

> If you will indeed obey My voice and keep My
> covenant, then you shall be a special treasure to
> Me above all people; for all the earth is Mine.
> And you shall be to Me a kingdom of priests and
> a holy nation.
>
> —Exodus 19:5–6 NKJV

This chapter begins with a war between two groups of kings. When a group ruled over another group in this period, it was primarily for the sake of collecting taxes and local resources from them. Sodom and Gomorrah had been under the "rule" and taxation of a king from the east and were ready to regain their independence. The ruling king from the east and his friends came to crush the rebellion, with the battle beginning somewhere near the Dead Sea. The ruling king won and kept ruling. To make an example out of these city-states, he raided the rebellious cities of the plain, including Sodom.

In the last chapter, we read that Lot had chosen this lush plain near Sodom and Gomorrah to dwell with his possessions. It would seem that Lot had become friends with the people of Sodom and had now moved into the city. While we have yet to be told of Sodom's evil ways, Lot's transition into the city tells us that he has gotten used to their evil ways. He was trusting more in man's protections and comforts than he was trusting in God. When the city was sacked, Lot was kidnapped along with the rest of the city. When Abram heard about his nephew's capture, he decided to rescue him. Abram had won the loyalty of many of his neighbors; three neighboring Amorite brothers joined Abram in the rescue. God had abundantly blessed Abram with 318 fighting men in his own household besides the Amorite brothers. Abram had now become a king of sorts with his own little army. With the promise that God was on his side, Abram chased down these kings from the East for over two hundred miles, defeated four kings and their armies in a surprise attack, and rescued the people of Sodom and their stuff. You know, when Lot saw them, he said, "I'm with that guy!"

On their way back home, Abram stopped at Salem (likely Jerusalem), where the priest of God Most High shared a meal with Abram and blessed him, followed by Abram giving him 10 percent of the redeemed plunder. This account is the first time a priest is mentioned in the Bible. Our repeated decisions to "eat the fruit" continue to separate us from God. A priest is someone who has dedicated their life to serve as an intermediary between the people and God. While not much is said about this priest, both David and the author of Hebrews will later make a significant point that since Abram recognized that this priest of God was greater than he, there is another "priesthood" that is greater than the Levitical priesthood (descendants of Abraham) that will develop in the next book. While God initiated the Levitical priesthood, it is only temporary until a greater priest arrives who can actually fix the sin problem rather than just remind us of the problem.

Then, the king of Sodom went to Abram and told him to keep the plunder in payment but asked Abram to return the Sodomites to Sodom. The king of Sodom obviously served a different god made in his own image, but here, Abram told the king, "No, I serve the real God who created everything, and I have promised Him that I will not keep your stuff. God has given me the best, and He doesn't want you to take any credit for what He has done and is going to do for me." Why would God care what the king of Sodom thought? Because God was using Abram to witness to this king about the character of God. Abram had been a lifesaver for this city in the image of the Life-Giver. God was telling the king and people of Sodom to serve Him and allow Him to determine what was right and wrong. God was using Abram to bless them and to try to save them from themselves. This reason was God's purpose in choosing Abram to bless all the other nations by mirroring the character of God.

REFLECTION QUESTIONS:

Remember how we said that sin breaks relationships with God and others? Following God does the opposite. When we really follow God, we will naturally build healthy relationships with others. Abram has developed a good relationship with his Amorite neighbors. What do you think God wants you to do to build better relationships?

_____

_____

_____

_____

_____

Why do you think God didn't want Abram to keep the plunder from Sodom?

_____

_____

_____

_____

_____

God was using Abram to witness to the leader of Sodom. What does this say about who God is?

_____

_____

_____

_____

_____

GENESIS 15

G enesis 1–11 sets up the problem with us and our broken world. Genesis 12 through the end of Revelation is God addressing this problem. God can't take the evil out of this broken world without also taking us humans out of it. There must be a radical change in us, in our relationship with God, and a remedy for all the death, destruction, and decay inflicted on the whole of creation.[33] God's calling and covenant with Abram is the beginning of God's plan to breathe His life back into the fabric of His creation.

Abram's ancestors tried to make a great name for themselves at the Tower of Babel, but instead, they had a lame name. Remember those poor, "confused" people? God then pulled out one of their descendants and told Abram that He would make a great name for Him.

At first, there seems to be a lot of repetition between God and

Abram's interactions over the last several chapters, but God has been growing Abram into the kind of man who can lead his family. Humans often see efficiency as the main goal for success, but God sees developing people into His character as the primary goal. God isn't in this thing to just "get the job done" but to develop us into the kind of beings who are worth living with for eternity. It takes a lot more work and heartache on His part, but He is committed to His creation and to their redemption. This idea right here is worth remembering when we are stressed out about life. God is in complete control, but He is using our stress to grow our character so that we become like Him. This concept kills the idea that the "end justifies the means" because God is more concerned that we make the right choices in the journey than about us arriving at a certain destination in this life.[34] Those choices are what make us into the kind of beings who can be life keepers and givers for eternity.

When God first spoke to Abram in this chapter, He said, "I gave you fear to protect you from evil and death, but if you follow the Life-Giver, you don't have to fear because I am your protection. I am everything you truly desire." Abram responded, "Um, no, I haven't had a child yet." God replied, "I am the Life-Giver. You and everyone else will be blown away when you see the life that I will give you. Trust Me, and don't try to figure this out on your own." For the first time in the book so far, the text notes that Abram believed in God. Verse 6 (NKJV) is one of the most powerful statements in the Bible: "And he [Abram] believed in the Lord, and He [the Lord] accounted it to him for righteousness."

What pleases God? How do we live righteously? A belief that God is who He says He is, that He will do what He says He will do, and that we are who God says we are. While our faith and trust in God results in good works, good works alone are not what pleases Him.[35]

In response to Abram's faith, God formalized His promise to Abram with a culturally relevant practice. From our perspective, Abram was asked to do something weird with animals. Today, when we buy property, we have our own cultural rituals, such as checking the financial background, going through the loan process, or signing the deed in the presence of a notary. The specific practice God and Abram performed here reflected a similar initiation ceremony of a land-grant treaty.[36]

By walking between the sacrifices, the covenant was being enacted with God promising the land to an unborn people and a curse upon Himself should the treaty ever be broken. As God cannot lie and cannot break His word,[37] the purpose of this ceremony was to demonstrate to Abram in a culturally relevant way God's seriousness in using his family to bring about the redemption of humanity, beginning with a place for them to call home. Abram could rest, knowing that not only would He have a biological heir, but his descendants would also become great people whom God would continue to look out for and eventually use to save the rest of the world.

Interestingly, God did not permit Abram to complete his side of the treaty ceremony. While God had expectations for Abram's family, He knew the heart of the man and how quickly we falter. Therefore, this covenant that God made rests entirely on Him. It's relatively easy to trust God when times are good and the sky is clear, but it's another matter if we will continue to trust God when times are hard and when it's difficult to see ahead. The question is, will Abram continue to trust God and His promise, or will He falter when trials come?

At the end of this ceremony, God revealed to Abram that his children would grow into a nation, be enslaved for a long time, and then come out richer than they went in. When God sets us free from anything, He doesn't barely get us out; we always come out richer and more whole than we were before we were in bondage. While Abram's family would face challenges in the coming years, we will see how God used those difficulties to cultivate and develop Abram's family into His own special people. Whoever God sets free has a new life breathed into them that they never had before.

This covenant is now the second God has made in the book. God's first covenant was with Noah and his children that He would never again destroy the earth. The second focuses on providing a home for Abram's family through whom He will redeem His creation.

REFLECTION QUESTIONS:

Why doesn't God just give us what He promises immediately? Wouldn't it be easier on God and us this way?

_____

_____

_____

_____

_____

God is showing us that He is willing to invest in the process of building our character through difficult times, as character is more important than our comfort. What does this say about who God is? What uncomfortable situations in your life is God using to develop your character right now?

_____

_____

_____

_____

_____

God credited Abram's faith as righteousness. If you truly believe what God says, how would that affect your actions and attitudes?

_____

_____

_____

_____

_____

GENESIS 16

We left chapter 15 feeling excited about Abram's faith and confidence in God and His promises. Several years pass between chapters 15 and 16. In this chapter, Abram and Sarai eat the fruit, believing they need to take matters into their own hands to help God fulfill His promise. Waiting on God to deliver His promise is a test of Abram's faith. How much does Abram actually trust God? It's easy to trust when things are going well; it's another thing to trust God when things don't seem to be working out.

When Abram and Sari first followed God's leading into Canaan, Sari was around sixty-five. By chapter 16, she was around seventy-five, and she recognized that her window for having kids was closed. Sari looked around and saw how her neighbors solved this kind of problem. She used her servant as a surrogate through whom she and Abram could have a child.[38] However, just because something is "acceptable" in your culture doesn't mean that God is okay with it. The first we heard of someone having more than one wife was the evil Lamech, a descendant of Cain, who boasted about killing people for no reason. Remember him? Well, now God's man, Abram, was going to try a similar stunt. Not a good idea, but once Abram questioned who God was, the bad ideas kept coming. The next thing we see is Abram having a baby with another woman.

Abram didn't actually do a lot of things right in the Bible, but on occasions, God was pleased with him because of Abram's faith. This event was not one of those times. The snake tempted Abram and Sari with the same garden temptation, "Is God really who He says He is? Are you really who He says you are?" Just like in the garden, Sari ate the fruit and convinced her husband to eat it as well. Abram's faith in God's promise failed here, and he decided that God needed help fulfilling his promises. So Abram helped God in finding a way to bless himself. When we doubt God and try to do His job in our own strength, there are always long-term consequences.

Abram slept with Hagar, his wife's maid, and she got pregnant. Abram was called to imitate God in giving life and protecting life. God's view of giving life to another is sacrificing ourselves for their mental, emotional, physical, and spiritual well-being. This was God's design for the sexual relationship between Adam and Eve. They had different abilities but equal value. The combination of both of them was the image of God. God's image was not complete until there was a covenant relationship where each partner sought the other's well-being above their own for as long as they lived. Here, we see that Abram violated Hagar emotionally, physically, spiritually, and mentally (albeit "culturally" appropriate). He used Hagar, but when his wife became upset with her, Abram abandoned Hagar. Abram went into this relationship with the intention of using Hagar to get something, knowing that he would never give her what she needed in return. This action is exactly the opposite of who God is and how He designed the sexual relationship.

God had already made a covenant with Abram, promising He would bless Abram and his descendants. God found Hagar in the desert and told her she would have a son. She was to call his name Ishmael, which literally translates as "God hears." God told her that because of His promise to Abram, her descendants would also grow into a large number. Ishmael would also inherit and live in the land that God had promised to Abram's descendants, but there would be regular tension and conflict with Abram's other descendants. God then sent her back to Abram. Even though Abram was not faithful to God or Hagar in this account, the God who sees and hears all remained faithful to Abram, to His promises, and to Hagar.

When we determine that we will define right and wrong for ourselves, we spread an infectious disease through all our relationships. That infection continues to grow in people and has consequences. Many Christians think that when we get saved, God not only takes away all our sins but also takes away all our consequences and gives us a clean new slate. While God does remove the infection and sin out of our hearts, He often doesn't undo the history we created. While God can redeem our poor choices, our actions often have lasting consequences. God is a great Redeemer who can turn around any situation, but He doesn't take away the freedom for humans to make their own choices. Once we have spread the disease, it is up to each person to decide what they will do with the infection we have given them. They can ask the Life-Giver to heal them, or they can continue to grow and spread that same infection. We can learn from the mistakes of Abram and Sari and choose to accept God's definition of right and wrong right now. God wants to transform us into people who spread healing and life instead of death, pain, and brokenness.

REFLECTION QUESTIONS:

In reflecting on your own Christian experience, how have you seen God redeem your blunders? While God has forgiven our sins, what type of consequences do you continue to experience from your own life choices or from the choices of others' past mistakes?

_____

_____

_____

_____

_____

Abram and Sari sought a culturally acceptable alternative to fix their situation. What are some "culturally acceptable" means you or other Christians are tempted to utilize that fall short of God's plan and purposes?

_____

_____

_____

_____

GENESIS 17

I n the previous chapter, Abram was eighty-six; by chapter 17, he was ninety-nine. Thirteen years have gone by since Ishmael was born. It seems as if Abram had accepted Ishmael as his promised descendant from God, but now, God was telling Abram, "Live in my image, submit to what I say is right and wrong, and be a life-giver and life nurturer. I haven't fulfilled what I promised you yet. You will still be the father of a great nation. Ishmael is not the one I promised you."

Abram thought it was ridiculous for him to have a kid fourteen years ago, so what about now? The book of Hebrews says that Abram's seed was as good as dead.[39] Some think that this means that both Sarah and Abram were past the point where it was physically possible for them to have kids. God waited until there could be no accident and no one else could take credit for this miracle. God was looking to build Abram into a man of faith. Faith that trusts God even when it becomes very uncomfortable.

Abram asked God to hear him and make a line out of Ishmael. Think about this. God already named Ishmael "God sees/God hears." Then God told Abram that He had already heard him and had already blessed Ishmael. God was telling him, "Thirteen years ago, I heard what you are saying now. You threw him out of your house, and I sent him back to bless him. Now, you are asking me to bless him. I'm way ahead of you. Stop trying to manipulate the situation, and trust me. You are worried that you and your wife are too old to have children, but I am the God of life, and I have already told you I would give you everything you need."

God is the creator of time, and He is outside of it. God hears our future prayers and knows what we need years down the road. We must learn to believe that "He works everything for good to those who love Him and are called according to His purpose" (Romans 8:28) if we are going to trust Him completely.

God then reaffirmed His covenant with Abram. There are many aspects to a covenant, so let's dive in and discuss some mentioned here. One of the main things we see in every covenant is some sort of blood that finalizes the commitment. In each of the covenants we have seen so far, an animal sacrifice was made until this one. This covenant calls for circumcision. What in the world is that about? Every male who was eight days old or older was to be circumcised. Circumcision wasn't the end goal; it was a symbol. The process is gross and painful, but the hell they were growing inside them was also gross and painful. God wanted them to understand that they were born with something in their hearts that needed to be taken out for them to really reflect His image. Circumcision was a sign to them and everyone else that they belonged to the God of Abram. It was a statement of faith that one day, God would also circumcise their hearts and take the hell out of them. God did not give Abram his promised son until Abram and every male in his "kingdom" was circumcised.

God made it clear that anyone who did not get circumcised was choosing not to follow the God of Abram. Therefore, they would no longer receive the promises given to Abram's descendants.

Another aspect of covenants is that God doesn't make the covenant with just one person. With both Noah and Abram, we see that the covenant lives on with their descendants. We often think of vows being "till death," but God's promises are *beyond* death. He is eternal, and so are all His promises. Stop and let that sink in. As human beings, we struggle to comprehend eternity because we live in a world where everything has an endpoint; but with God, there is no end! So when we try to comprehend eternity, we really can't grasp it, but all of God's promises will last longer than we can imagine.

We also see that in a covenant, each partner takes on the relationship and alliances of the other. Later in this book, God protects Lot because God has an alliance with Abram. We see God bless Ishmael because of Abram's relationship with Hagar. Anyone who sides with Abram will also be blessed by God.

Then God changed Abram's name from Abram to Abraham. Abram means "exalted father."[40] Abraham means "father of a multitude."[41] How do you become a father? By giving life and reproducing in your image. How do you become a *good* father? By being committed to nurturing that life. So his name went from being a "life-giver and nurturer" to "life-giver and nurturer of many." Could it be any more obvious that God really wanted Abraham to represent God's character to the rest of the world? He is literally naming Abraham after Himself. Not only did Abraham's name change, but God's name also took on Abraham's. From this point on, when God introduces Himself, He often calls Himself the God of Abraham. Abraham and God are forever tied. Abraham's identity has forever changed, and God's reputation is now in the hands of Abraham and his descendants.

Let's take a moment to notice a little detail in God's covenant with Abraham that is easily overlooked. God also gave each of

Abraham's servants and slaves the opportunity to enter into the covenant. If they chose to accept the terms of the covenant, God was ready to elevate everyone in Abraham's service to the privileges that He was giving to Abraham's descendants. God was offering everyone a chance at this new freedom because His desire is that everyone would choose to reflect Him as the Life-Giver. God was elevating the role of Abraham's servants and slaves to members of Abraham's family. Treating all humanity with respect and value was a big part of reflecting the character of the Life-Giver.

REFLECTION QUESTIONS:

God has talked to Abraham four times about His plan for Abraham's life. Why does God need to keep reminding him of His promise and the need for Abraham to follow God's definition of right and wrong? Does God have to keep reminding you of anything? We are forgetful, impatient beings. What can we do to help remind ourselves of God's promises and His definition of right and wrong in our own lives?

_____

_____

_____

_____

_____

When we enter into a marriage with someone, God intended for us to enter into a covenant relationship (not a contract). What are some of the different aspects of a covenant brought out in this chapter? How might these also apply to marriage? If you are married, how could you better strengthen this covenant relationship? If you are single, how does this affect the qualities you look for in a potential spouse?

_____

_____

_____

_____

Think about God being outside of time. He knows the end from the beginning. How does that change your relationship with Him?

_____

_____

_____

_____

GENESIS 18

We have a lot going on here! The events in this chapter likely took place about three months after the renewal of the covenant and the circumcisions in the previous chapter. God told Abraham that he should prepare to have a son very soon. Judging by Abraham's attitude, he seemed to realize that He was talking with God or God's divine messenger. Some think this could have been Jesus appearing to Abraham. Abraham was taking them seriously and giving them all he could think to give them. Both Sarah and Abraham were past the point in life where they could have babies. Sarah was eavesdropping on the conversation from inside the tent. She was listening and processing the information and was having a silent conversation in her head. She thought it was ridiculous and found it funny that she should have a baby in her old age.

Apparently, she hadn't believed Abraham when he had told

her the news. In the midst of her silent conversation, the Lord told Abraham what Sari said in her thoughts, and the Lord held her accountable. Up to this point, humans were held accountable for their actions; but now, God was also holding her accountable for her secret thoughts and attitudes. Even dwelling on doubts about God's promises leads to problems. Do you see the snake tempting Sarah with the same old doubts and questions? "Is God really who He says He is? Are you really who He says you are? Is God capable of giving you a son? Are you capable of being a mother?" Once again, she repeated the garden story by doubting God. When the Lord asked what she had done, she hid and covered it up.

Then God told Abraham that he planned to see what was happening in Sodom. God had heard the cries of the abused and the afflicted, and He was going to see if the city was truly as wicked as it sounded. If it was, then He would destroy the city. Why did God have to come to see the city if He knew all things? God was doing this for the sake of His relationship with Abraham. He had made a covenant to be an ally with Abraham's allies. Lot was one of Abraham's allies, so God was honoring their covenant.

Why would God destroy an entire city? God said He had heard their cries of pain and was going to put an end to their suffering. One day, I was cooking dinner and cutting up a lot of vegetables with a five-inch-long knife. One of my two-year-olds saw the pretty, shiny knife and decided he wanted it. Whenever I turned my back, he would try to get that knife. I kept trying to keep him from getting it because I knew if he got it, there was no limit to the amount of pain and suffering he could inflict on himself, his twin, and his siblings. He had no idea how dangerous his desire for that knife was, but I did.

In the Garden of Eden, Adam and Eve reached out and grasped something much more dangerous than any knife. They grabbed the power to create hell in their hearts and began using it to stab themselves and each other. God heard the cries of pain coming from this city as they were torturing one another. He had already given them a chance to change and follow the God of Abraham when he rescued them from their enemies a couple of chapters ago. God had helped Abraham rescue them and then met Abraham with instructions on how to witness and reach out to them, and yet, they wanted to keep deciding good and evil for themselves. Their cries broke God's heart, and He decided to end the city's evil and pain infliction.

What was up with Abraham's long conversation with the Lord? Abraham obviously thought there were more righteous people in the city than there were. With each negotiation, Abraham realized he was wrong about the righteous in the city. Abraham's desire was to save Lot and Lot's household. Remember how Lot had a large household and was very wealthy? He had lots of people who worked for him. Abraham assumed that Lot had been a righteous man who had led his household to follow the God of Abraham, but with each decrease in number, the reality hit Abraham. Lot's household wasn't righteous after all, and maybe Lot wasn't either. He finally gave up in the end because he realized that the Lord would save the righteous, but there might not be any righteous people left in Sodom.

REFLECTION QUESTIONS:

Sometimes we're tempted to think that our secret thoughts and attitudes don't really matter to God or others. They don't really hurt anyone, right? However, God called attention to Sarah's secret thoughts and attitudes. Why do our secret thoughts matter?

_____

_____

_____

_____

_____

When confronted with the prospect of Sodom, Gomorrah, and the cities of the plain being destroyed, Abraham was moved with compassion for their inhabitants, as sinful as they might be. What kind of attitude should we have toward those who live in sin today?

_____

_____

_____

_____

_____

GENESIS 19

W ow! This chapter has some very disturbing things in it! Why is this in the Bible anyway? This chapter opens with the servants of God coming to Sodom to see the city. Lot greeted them with wonderful hospitality and invited them to stay with him. A mob of men from the city came to Lot's house and demanded that Lot give over his male guests so that the mob of men could rape them. Lot recognized that this demand was wicked, and he tried to protect his guests. In his desire to protect his guests, he offered his virgin daughters for these men to abuse however they wanted. The mob didn't want the virgin girls; they wanted to rape the men. The mob decided to break down the door, kidnap the visitors and Lot, and do whatever they wanted with them. Wild story!

The whole scenario is appalling—from the mob's actions to Lot's response. Why is this even in the Bible? God is telling us what kind of city this was. First of all, where were the police or the ones who protect the innocent? It seems there was no justice system, and evil ruled in this city. If this was happening to adults, what was happening to the children? God said He had heard their cries of agony and their broken, evil hearts.

The angels protected Lot and told him to gather everyone who would go with him. Lot didn't seem to have much influence over his family as he tried to convince his household to leave. Lot had been a wealthy man, so he had lots of people in his care; but when he left, he only had his wife and two of his daughters. There were several times when God tried to pull Lot out of Sodom, but he couldn't pull Sodom out of Lot. Remember the time when Lot was kidnapped and rescued by Abraham? He still went back to Sodom. After Lot left Abraham, the Bible mentions several times that there was plenty of land closer to Abraham, but Lot still wanted Sodom. First, Lot had pitched his tent toward Sodom; then he moved to Sodom; then Sodom was his family. Lot was embraced by very wicked people and even became a city council member. He was a torn person. Lot knew and wanted to do what was right, but he didn't want to leave the comforts of this city of sin. This divided heart led him to make bad choices. He was willing to protect strangers (which is good), but he was willing to give his daughters away to be gang-raped (very bad!), and all this to appease his neighbors. He had put himself in a situation where he didn't have good options.

Even when the angels told Lot and his family to leave, the family kept lingering. The angels literally grabbed Lot's hand, his wife's hand, and each of his girl's hands and dragged them from the city. When the angel told them where to go to safety, Lot said, "I don't want to go there. I'll die. I want to go to another city." He still wanted to enjoy the city life with its comforts and security. The angels said okay and told them not to look back because this would show that they weren't willing to leave the life of sin. God was rescuing them so they could live righteously away from the sinful city, but looking back would prove they weren't willing to leave the Sodom life behind and would end up spreading it wherever they went. Lot's wife looked back and immediately became a pillar of salt. In Luke, Jesus mentions Lot's wife, saying that she wanted to preserve her life, but she lost it. Even though she was dragged out of the city, her heart never left Sodom.

Lot had wanted to go to a city, but God told him to go to the mountains. God agreed to keep Lot safe in the city, but when Lot saw what God had done to Sodom and Gomorrah, he got scared and went to the mountains. Here, we see the snake again, asking Lot if God is really who He says He is and if Lot really is who God says he is. Lot didn't seem to trust that God was really going to destroy Sodom, or he wouldn't have been lingering. Then Lot didn't trust God to get him to the mountains; then he didn't trust God not to destroy the little town of Zoar.

Once again, we see the torn Lot, who didn't like evil, but he loved his comfort. He didn't really trust God because he didn't know God. Whenever we don't trust in God, it is because we don't really *know* Him or aren't willing to surrender to His outcome.

Lot had lost a lot. He lost his position, his home, his wife, some of his children who wouldn't leave, his servants, and his possessions. His daughters were so traumatized by the events that they believed that they were the sole survivors on earth. Like their father, they lacked trust in God, so they took matters into their own hands and got their father so drunk that he didn't even know what was going on. The daughters then had sex with their father, and each became pregnant. Both of their families grew to become wicked nations that we will run into later in the biblical story. What Lot's daughters did was absolutely repulsive, but Lot made his home in a city that glorified degrading sexual practices. Now, Lot had lost all his children to Sodom's definition of good and evil. Lot was willing to sacrifice his daughters' sexual purity to protect himself and his household. Then, his daughters turned around and sacrificed their sexual purity to protect themselves and their household.

Lot was not an amazing man, but this story isn't about Lot; it is about God. God is still honoring his covenant with Abraham. God was blessing Lot because Abraham cared for him. God and Abraham are now on the same side, so anyone Abraham blesses, God also blesses.

REFLECTION QUESTIONS:

"Bad company corrupts good character."[42] How do you see this proverb applying to Lot and his family? How have you seen this proverb apply in your own life or in the lives of those around you?

_____

_____

_____

_____

_____

We prioritize what we value. What does Lot seem to prioritize and value? As you look at your own life, what would others think that you prioritize? Consider asking a few close friends their honest opinions about what seems to be the priorities in your life. What needs to change to help you better prioritize your trust and faith in God?

_____

_____

_____

_____

_____

Hurt people hurt people. Lot hurt his daughters; his daughters hurt him, and the family dysfunction grew into a warped nation. We just continue the cycle. In the power of Christ, how can you help to reverse the trend in your sphere of influence?

_____

_____

_____

_____

_____

GENESIS 20

Old habits die hard. Just when we were getting excited about what God was doing in Abraham's life, Abraham blew it. For whatever reason, Abraham decided to move to Gerar and then realized he was afraid of King Abimelech. And here we go again. Not only did he convince Sarah to say she was his sister instead of his wife, but Abraham also confessed this had been his standard practice. How many other times had Abraham done this? The Bible mentions two times, but it sounds like a well-rehearsed story. Technically, it's true; she was his half sister, but Sarah was also his wife. Abraham was trading his wife off like property once again to protect himself. Can I just say here that Sarah must have been one pretty lady? She was at least ninety years old, and Abraham knew the king would want her as soon as he saw her! When God says he is going to bless you, He does! But back to the story. Here comes that snake again. "Is God really who He says He is? Are you really who God says you are?"

Do you remember when God told Abraham not to be afraid of anyone? God said He is the Life-Giver and Sustainer. He would protect Abraham and be everything he desired. One of the first consequences we experience when we don't trust God is a lack of discernment.

If you really want to see others for who they are, you must first know who God is. Abraham did not trust God, so he misjudged Abimelech. In his paranoia, Abraham jumped to conclusions about Abimelech's character, but Abraham was completely wrong. Abimelech acted *more* righteous than Abraham in this account. Abraham had forgotten that God had promised to be Abraham's shield and protector. Abraham had forgotten who he was and who God was.

Abraham was scared for his life and was sacrificing his wife (along with the promised seed) to save himself—*again.* Abraham walked into this land and basically said Abimelech didn't live by God's view of right and wrong, so he shouldn't either. The ironic thing is that Abimelech acted more morally than Abraham. Because Abimelech feared God, he wouldn't take Sarah to be his wife. Abimelech recognized that God was on Abraham's side, so he gave Abraham gifts to appease Abraham and his God.

The tragedy here is that Abimelech received a bad view of the image of God. God was not okay with Abraham's selfish behavior, but Abimelech's view of the true God was being shaped by Abraham's actions. Abimelech saw Abraham's God as a punk out to get him. Abraham's selfishness hurt God and Abimelech's relationship with God. People form their ideas about God from the actions of those following Him.

Not only had Abraham wronged Sarah and Abimelech, but Abraham was also putting God's plan in jeopardy. God had promised Abraham that his wife was going to have a baby who would be the father of many nations, but Abraham traded in that wife for some temporary security. We don't know if Sarah was pregnant at that time, but if Abraham had lost her, he would have lost his promise from God. What if Abimelech had taken Sarah as his wife and assumed the child was his? Abraham was destroying his future and making some really foolish choices based on his fear. The fear that God had already told him not to have!

In this account, Abraham was an embarrassing failure to God. God told Abimelech that he had chosen Abraham to be His prophet. Abimelech feared Abraham's mighty God, but Abraham feared Abimelech's army. *However*, this isn't a story about Abraham; this is a story of God's faithfulness. God rescued not only Abraham and Sarah but also His promise to Abraham's descendants. Why did Abraham go to Gerar in the first place? Abraham already had or had been promised everything that he could have wanted. Abraham hijacked God's plan for his life and got himself in a weird mess, but God was faithful and came to his rescue—again.

REFLECTION QUESTIONS:

In the last chapter, both Lot and his daughters use sex to advance their own security and agendas. Here, we see Abraham doing the same thing! How do people today use sex in similar ways?

Sometimes, like Abraham, we convince ourselves that half-truths are morally acceptable, but are deceitful half-truths really any better than a lie? About what kinds of things are you tempted to tell half-truths? How do you think our view of God affects the way we are tempted to be misleading in these areas?

_____

_____

_____

_____

_____

People's understanding of God comes largely from the behavior of His people. For many, you may well be the only "Bible" they ever read. From your own attitudes, actions, and conversations (and your social media posts and comments) this past week, what would be their perception of who your God is?

_____

_____

_____

_____

Abraham prioritized the temporal challenges over God's long-term plan. How are you tempted to let the day-to-day challenges overshadow the bigger picture of what God wants to do in your life? What are some areas you need to learn to trust God?

_____

_____

_____

_____

_____

GENESIS 21

God always fulfills His promises. After leaving Haran a quarter of a century before, Abraham became a father at the age of one hundred, and Sarah became a mother at the age of ninety. God's promise had been a long time coming. Around twenty-five years have passed since God first made this promise to Abraham. Both Abraham and Sarah had laughed in disbelief when God said they would have a child, so God told them to name their son Isaac, the Hebrew word for *laughter*. At first, Abraham and Sarah's laughter was sarcastic disbelief, but after the birth of their son, their laughter was filled with joy at the miracle of God.

Some of God's promises are dependent or conditional on something we do. For example, 2 Chronicles 7:14 (NKJV) is a conditional promise: "If My people … will humble themselves, and pray and seek My face, and turn from their wicked ways, then I ...will forgive their sin and heal their land." Other promises are unconditional, meaning that God will do it even if we are unfaithful because God keeps His promises. This promise to Abraham was fulfilled not because of what Abraham did but because God made an unconditional promise.

The account then skips ahead a couple of years. At this time, Isaac was between two to five years old, and Ishmael was between fifteen and eighteen. The text says that Ishmael "laughed" at Laughter (Isaac), but we get the impression this wasn't a "you're a funny toddler" kind of laugh but a mocking or bullying kind of laugh. Obviously, this angered Mama Sarah. Sarah wanted to make Hagar leave, but Abraham was hesitant. Abraham seems to have genuinely cared for Ishmael. Abraham sought God in this difficult situation. Way to go, Abraham! Good move. God told Abraham to listen to Sarah and have Ishmael leave. God promised Abraham that God would still bless and care for Ishmael, but Ishmael was not the child through whom all peoples of the earth would be blessed. Perhaps Abraham's hesitancy was because he wanted a backup plan in case Isaac didn't work out, but God made it clear that God didn't need Abraham's help again.

Keep in mind that the conflict came from Ishmael to Isaac. In Galatians, Paul talks about this conflict as an illustration of the conflict between those who follow God and sinful people bullying followers of God. In Galatians 4, some Jewish people were telling non-Jewish followers of Jesus that because they weren't descendants of Abraham, they couldn't be blessed by God. Paul told the Jewish people that they thought they were descendants of Isaac, but they were really descendants of Ishmael in their hearts because they were promoting racism and bondage to legalism. He told them that followers of Jesus are also part of the promised line because of faith. This story isn't about a special genetic line that God blessed; it is an illustration that we can all be blessed by God if we choose to believe in Him. It is all up to us, not our heritage.

God was using this as an illustration for Abraham's

descendants to see that to follow God, we must completely abandon ourselves to His definition of right and wrong. Ishmael was an example of Abraham's selfishness and distrust of God. God was telling him that the selfishness and distrust had to go. There is no way we can have both our selfishness and our faith living in us without a constant war. We have to be free of the selfishness that wars with God.

So was God rejecting Ishmael? No, God still had plans to protect and bless Ishmael, but it was not through Ishmael that God was going to bring the redemption of His creation. He might not have been chosen for God's special plan, but Ishmael was not rejected from being in a relationship with God. While God would bless Ishmael and his family solely for Abraham's sake, a relationship with God would be dependent on Ishmael. It can look like God was being really harsh by allowing Abraham to send him away, but God is telling us that we have to be really harsh with the selfishness that is warring in our hearts against God. Why didn't Abraham give Hagar more? Abraham realized it was God who would make them prosper. God had already promised to do this. No matter what Abraham gave to them, it would never be enough. God had to be the one to meet their needs now, and He would give them more than Abraham ever could.

After they wandered through the desert, it wasn't long before Hagar and Ishmael were totally dependent upon God for their survival. Look how God responded to Ishmael's cry for help. God's promise to Ishmael echoed the promise God gave to Abraham. He said, "Don't be afraid. I will take care of you. I am going to make a great nation from your line." And He did. God not only provided for their immediate need for water, but God's presence also remained with Ishmael as he grew and developed. Let's be clear. God was not against Ishmael and his kids. God desired for them to prosper, and they did. Ishmael is considered the father of many of the Arab people.

After several years passed, the text picked up with a strange encounter with Abimelech. The word Abimelech means "my father is king,"[43] so it is more of a Canaanite title than a personal name. This individual might or might not be the same Abimelech from the last chapter. If this is the same Abimelech, notice the change. Abraham had approached Abimelech as an unknown nomadic family, but now, King Abimelech sought out Abraham as an equal. Abimelech saw that God was blessing Abraham and wanted a guarantee from Abraham that he wouldn't trick him and his descendants. He wanted to be buddies. Abraham said, "Deal, but by the way, let's clear up a problem. I dug a well, and your people took it." Abimelech claimed to know nothing about it and gave it back over to Abraham in exchange for some sheep to serve as a reminder of the deal. After Abimelech left, Abraham planted a tree to seal the deal and talked to God.

What does this have to do with anything? Abraham named the well Beersheba, meaning "well of the oath." First, God had been faithful in blessing Abraham, granting him favor with the locals and establishing Abraham and his family in the land just as He had promised. Beersheba will also become an important landmark as the southern border town of the land of Israel in the rest of the biblical story. This little blip gives us some background to how this town was first started and to whom it belongs.

REFLECTION QUESTIONS:

God took Abraham and Sarah's bitterness and turned it into joy. How has God taken your bitterness and distress and turned it into joy? What are some things in your life that really bring you joy? All good things are ultimately a gift from God. How are these gifts ultimately from Him?

_____

_____

_____

_____

God took away Abraham's backup plan for a descendant. Has God ever taken away your backup plan so you would learn to trust Him?

_____

_____

_____

_____

GENESIS 22

What in the world is going on here? So now the God of life wants human sacrifices?

God has been working with Abraham to build him into the kind of man who would live by faith and who would influence his family to follow God. God had been patiently leading and teaching Abraham year after year for nearly forty-five years. Abraham had everything that he wanted. Would Abraham be willing to follow God, or would he start *eating the fruit* now that he had it all? God asked Abraham to give up what would cost him the most before He would give him his future descendants. In the life of every true believer, God will also ask us to surrender what we hold most dear.

God is not satisfied until we are *all in* because He is *all in.* If we hold anything back, the relationship can never be what it is meant to be. Imagine getting married, and your partner says,

"I am all yours except for one other person. I will spend most of my time, my life, and my money on you, except for 5 percent that I will give to this other person." No sane person would commit to a relationship like that unless they are also holding back. God is letting us know that He is giving us His all, He is not holding Himself back, and we can't either.

Why does God call Isaac Abraham's only son? Because Isaac was the only one who would continue God's covenant with Abraham. God was making it clear that He was not switching His covenant to Ishmael or any other person.

Sacrificing humans, especially children, to the Canaanite gods was a fairly common practice by the people who dwelled in the land of Canaan.[44] While this practice may have been "culturally acceptable," Abraham was surely surprised that His life-giving God would want something like this. After this trial, God made it clear He did *not* want this kind of sacrifice.

God is also letting us know that the end never justifies the means. Oftentimes, we trust in God's promises and then justify what we do to get them. However, God was telling Abraham that trusting in God was the most important thing and that God would work out the rest. God was infinitely capable of providing a descendant for Abraham, but God's goal was to develop Abraham into a father who would truly lead his family to surrender and follow the Life-Giver. It is about the relationship and who we become in the process, not what we accomplish. Rest in that when life doesn't seem to be "working out" or when you only seem to be spinning your wheels. God doesn't measure success the way we do. God doesn't need amazing buildings, lots of biblical literature, or preachers; but He chooses to call people to do these things to grow them into His image. God is using the struggles to transform us into beings who will be worth living with forever.

Reading Abraham's response makes us want to say, "Who are you, and what have you done with Abraham?" This man is not the same Abram who used his servant Hagar to get what he wanted or who traded his wife for security at least two times! Abraham got up early the next morning and immediately began to do what God had called him to do. He didn't understand, but he did it anyway. Abraham was not going to "help God out" and intervene this time. He didn't forget the knife at home or call in sick. He was going to trust God even if it cost him everything. This is a new Abraham.

Abraham did what God asked of him, even when he didn't feel like it. Like Abraham, we walk by faith, not by feelings. We get up and do what is right no matter how we may feel at the moment. It is dangerous for us to take the attitude that we aren't going to submit until we feel like it or understand it all. Seldom will we ever see the bigger picture, fully understand, or agree that the difficult path is best. King Abraham did it all himself without using his army. He saddled his own donkey, chopped the wood, and prepared for the journey. Then he went to "worship God." He spent three long days as he journeyed. Once he arrived, he told his servants in faith *we* will return because he believed in God's promise. Abraham believed that even if God had to raise Isaac from the dead, God would be faithful to His promise (Hebrews 11:17–19).

As we think about Abraham's faith in this passage, let's not forget Isaac! He wasn't just a bystander here! Often, we think of Isaac as a toddler; however, the timing suggests he was anywhere between the ages of seven and thirty-seven. Most likely, Isaac was a teenager or young man because he was capable of carrying a large amount of wood up the mountain. Whatever his age, he was probably stronger than his one-hundred-plus-year-old father. Isaac could easily have fought off his father, but the fact that he willingly allowed himself to be tied as a sacrifice shows that he had trust in his father and faith in his father's God. Twice, the passage says Abraham and Isaac "went on together," telling us that even after Isaac questioned the sacrifice, he still agreed to be a part of it. Isaac carried the wood used to sacrifice himself up the mountain.

While God might have provided a ram as a substitute for the moment, two thousand years later, the Lord would ultimately provide the perfect sacrifice in the person of our Savior Jesus. Jesus spent the night before his death questioning the sacrifice but then agreed with His Father to be a part of it. He carried the wood used to sacrifice Himself up this very same group of mountains.

The story of the Bible is like a beautiful flower that has roots poking through into every story in the Old Testament and then blooms in the New Testament. This story isn't just about Abraham or Isaac. This story is about Jesus and God's final plan to give us life again. Abraham saw this reality in naming the mountain Jehovah-Jireh (literally, The Lord Will Provide).[45] While Abraham recognized that God had provided a symbolic substitute for the moment, He also caught a glimpse ahead that God would ultimately provide a way for man to be reconciled to God and once again join heaven and earth together as it was intended to be in the Garden. This means would be how Abraham's seed would ultimately bless the world.

Abraham faced the garden snake again when he heard, "Is God really who He says He is?" and "Are you really who God says you are?" In this passage, Abraham accepted God's definition of good and evil. This response wasn't just a test for Abraham but a life-changing experience. He went from being a man who relied on himself to a man who surrendered to God. Now, he had burned his bridges, and he was going to trust God for the outcome and do it God's way. Abraham once again accepted God's promise. "I am His image, and He will be the Life-Giver to me and my descendants."

At this high moment of faith, the story suddenly switches to a list of Abraham's brother's family. Why this random change? Well, now that Abraham is the kind of man who can lead a nation, it is time to get on with the promised descendants. So coming soon: a wife for Isaac.

REFLECTION QUESTIONS:

Once Abraham started tying Isaac up, Isaac had a good idea of what was going on. Why do you think he went along with the plan?

_____

_____

_____

_____

It is easy for us to think that the end justifies the means, but God is showing us that He is more interested in developing our character than in achieving a certain goal. How does that change your thinking about God's will for your life?

_____

_____

_____

_____

Isaac represented all of Abraham's hopes and dreams for the future. God asked Abraham to give up the thing that was dearest to him, and He will ask you to give up what is dearest to you. But He may not give yours back. What is dearest to you, and are you willing to surrender it to God?

_____

_____

_____

_____

_____

GENESIS 23

Twenty years likely lapsed between the close of the last chapter and Sarah's death. Although she was not without her faults, Sarah was a remarkable woman. She was a devoted wife to Abraham, following his leadership as he followed God, even when it didn't make sense. At the age when most of us are ready to retire, Sarah set off on a new journey of faith, living as a nomad in a foreign country. Even from the age of sixty-five to one hundred, she was a beautiful lady. So much so that when Abraham's faith wavered, he ditched her to save his own skin, but Sarah still remained loyal to the plan Abraham had selfishly devised until God stepped in.

Being childless, Sarah carried a great weight on her shoulders. Undoubtedly, she blamed herself and God at times for the unfulfilled promise of an heir. In her despair and human reasoning, she manipulated Hagar and Abraham to conceive a son for her. After all, God hadn't explicitly said that she would be the mother of the multitude, right? Only that Abraham would be the father of one. The plan entirely backfired, leading to anger and resentment. It wasn't until Sarah was eighty-nine that God specifically mentioned her in connection with His covenant. Although she laughed at the prospect of having a child at the age of ninety, by faith, she trusted God and "judged Him faithful who had promised."[46] Interestingly, Sarah is the only woman whose age at death is recorded in the Bible. As Abraham is held up as a spiritual father of faith, Sarah is also commended for her godly example by Isaiah, Peter, Paul, and the author of Hebrews.

This chapter gives a long account of Sarah's death and Abraham's response, but why? This chapter shows us an appropriate response to the death of a loved one. Abraham has hope but acknowledged that death is wrong and sin has caused this tragedy. We were never meant to die, so it can never be easy.

By the time of Sarah's death, Abraham and his family had moved back to Hebron. This place was where he had previously built an altar and met with God. Although God had promised the land to Abraham's descendants, Abraham has only lived as a stranger and nomad in the land. It is here, just outside Hebron, that Abraham officially buys his first and only property in the Promised Land. This act establishes a permanent claim to the land for Abraham and his descendants.

Why are the details of this land deal recorded here? It has been over sixty years since God promised Abraham and his descendants this land, and now Abraham officially owns his first piece of real estate. The entire public transaction seems awkward to us, but it follows the Hittite's custom, so there would be no question that Abraham was the owner. It is unlikely that Ephron would have actually parted with the cave for free.[47] Had Abraham accepted the offer, Ephron's children would likely reclaim the land after their father's death. Instead, Abraham insists on purchasing the cave. In typical Middle Eastern diplomacy, Ephron makes it clear that the cave will only be sold with the entire field and its trees; then, he puts an exorbitant price tag on the property. Ephron is out to make some real money in this deal.

Although it would have been culturally acceptable for Abraham to haggle for a fair price, he refuses and decides to pay the full amount.[48] Now, no one can come back later and say that Abraham had cheated Ephron or his children out of their inheritance. The chapter closes with Abraham laying his beloved wife to rest in the cave. This cave will become a family cemetery for many of his descendants, including himself, his son, and his future grandson.

REFLECTION QUESTIONS:

This chapter gives us some insight into a godly man mourning the loss of his wife. How should godly people deal with the death of loved ones?

_____

_____

_____

_____

Abraham is God's image to Ephron and the Hittites. What does Abraham's deal with Ephron say about who Abraham is and about who God is?

_____

_____

_____

_____

_____

GENESIS 24

Just as God had promised, God had "blessed Abraham in all things." About three years after Sarah's death, Abraham wasn't getting any younger and was ready for some grandkids. (If God was going to bless all people through Abraham's promised family, grandkids and a wife for Isaac were kind of important!) Abraham asked his godly, trusted servant to go get his son a wife from Abraham's hometown. Why didn't Abraham want his son to marry a local Canaanite woman? Was Abraham racist? Abraham had seen the wicked things the Canaanites believed and practiced, and he wanted to ensure that he found his son a virtuous wife who would embrace God's definition of good and evil. Abraham knew her beliefs and character would greatly influence his son and their descendants.

Why did Abraham send a servant instead of his son? First, remember that this was a very different culture from ours, and arranged marriages were common. Second, Abraham was concerned that if his son returned, he might become too comfortable in Haran and decide it was a nice place to live instead of God's Promised Land. Abraham did all he could to ensure his son followed God and remained faithful to the covenant.

The road trip began. Abraham's most trusted servant (probably Eliezer) traveled around seven hundred miles one-way to get Isaac's bride. When Eliezer arrived, he felt the weight of the responsibility to find the right wife for Isaac and, by faith, called out to God for a sign.

So are circumstances a good way to determine God's will? We must remember that oftentimes, when we rely on this type of revelation, we can become very biased. We ignore what we don't like and pay attention to what we do like. When determining God's will, we need to see what scripture, experience, reason, tradition, and the advice of godly people also have to say about the issue. In this situation, though, Eliezer established the criteria before the encounter and not during, adding to the credibility. Note that Eliezer's sign had nothing to do with looks or chance. His request would reveal the woman's character. He was looking for someone willing to nurture life even if it was extra work, so he picked a test that would show her heart. Watering all his camels would probably be at least an hour of hard, heavy work, so anyone volunteering for it would have to be a special person. Custom and common courtesy would compel most to draw water for a visitor, but only someone with a compassionate heart would offer to draw up water for all these strangers' camels (likely fifty to three hundred gallons of water!)

Eliezer didn't help her; he just watched. Sounds kinda like a rude thing to do, but he wanted to see if she would actually carry through with it. Before Eliezer was done praying, God was answering his prayer. Eliezer, by faith, gave her jewelry because he believed she was the one. He went to her home and immediately made his offer to the family.

Here, we are introduced to Laban, who will become a significant character down the road. Eliezer told his story and the purpose of his quest. After the family agreed to the marriage, Eliezer gave her family gifts from the bridegroom according to the cultural custom. Eliezer insisted they stay just one night as he desired to take the bride home to his master. The family had agreed to the marriage but wanted more time with her. This extra time would give her and the family a chance to say goodbye. Let's face it, Rebekah was leaving with a complete stranger to a foreign land without any hope of returning. Kind of a big deal. Here, Rebekah spoke up, accepted the risk, and decided to leave immediately.

This can look like quite the whirlwind romance, but it was well planned out by God before the couple had a clue. Keep in mind that love is not a feeling but a choice. Isaac and Rebekah each chose to love each other before they ever knew each other. Isaac was in the field meditating, implying something like our idea of personal devotions with God. Rebekah covered her face as a cultural expression of purity, modesty, and submission.[49] God knew who they were on the inside and decided they were perfect for each other. They met and were married right away. The author makes it clear that Isaac truly loved his new bride, Rebekah.

REFLECTION QUESTIONS:

From this narrative, what can we discern about Rebekah's character? What aspects should we seek to imitate or look for in a spouse? How does Rebekah's character contrast with what society tells us we should be looking for in a spouse?

_____

_____

_____

Our society often pushes that love is a feeling, but the Bible shows us time and again that love is a choice. How do we choose to love someone when we don't feel like it?

_____

_____

_____

_____

_____

GENESIS 25

After Sarah's death and after Isaac married Rebekah, Abraham lived for another thirty-five years and married another woman, Keturah; and they had six more sons. Of course, each of Keturah's sons would become the fathers of nations also in the Palestine or Arabian regions.[50] Before Abraham died, he sent his other sons to another land and gave them gifts to ensure they did not take away from Isaac's inheritance.

Abraham died at the ripe old age of 175 years, about 100 years after God first called him from his home in Haran. Abraham was buried in the same cave as Sarah near Hebron. Abraham blew it many times, but God developed him into a man with mind-blowing faith. The New Testament mentions Abraham seventy times because God was proud of His friend. Abraham went from being the kind of person who used others to get what he wanted to the kind of man who sacrificed what he wanted for the good of others. Interestingly, both Isaac (aged seventy-five) and Ishmael (aged eighty-eight) bury their father together.

Before moving on to Isaac as the next focal point of the covenant, the text reminds us of God's fulfilled promise to Ishmael. We read how God had blessed Ishmael and kept His promises to Abraham. Ishmael now had twelve sons who became princes and fathers of nations. That is pretty cool!

The text then shifts to focus on Isaac's family. Like her mother-in-law, Rebekah also struggled to have children. After a twenty-year battle with infertility, God answered Isaac's prayer, and Rebekah became pregnant. After their long struggle to get pregnant, Rebekah was worried because she realized something was not normal about this baby. I know from experience that a twin pregnancy can make you feel like you are about to give birth to a raging octopus, so it is understandable that Rebekah lost her cool. She rightly took her concerns to God, who told her there was more than one person in her womb. Then God told her something unusual about her sons.

The younger one would be the one who carried the covenant promise, not the older one. In Romans, Paul tells us that God made this choice not because of their performance but because it was His sovereign will. In Malachi 1, in reference to the nations who would grow from these two sons, God says, "Jacob I have loved, Esau have I hated." This statement can be hard for us to understand, but if we interpret that according to Romans 9, it is more like "Jacob have I accepted, Esau have I rejected" to carry on the covenant promise. Neither Romans nor Malachi talked about individual salvation or God's love but God choosing to use one brother over the other to accomplish His divine plan. Later, we find out that God greatly blessed Esau, further proving that God was not against him. From a cultural perspective, one would expect God to have selected the firstborn. It can be hard to understand God's choices, but we must know that His choices come from a wisdom that sees all things, present and future. Our view is very limited, so we choose to trust in the goodness of His character when we don't understand.

Let's be honest. How Isaac and Rebekah named their children is a little strange. Esau was named for how he appeared red and hairy at birth. He seemed to be a man-baby the day he was born, and they decided he would always be known for it. Can you imagine his mom looking for her lost toddler, "Has anyone seen Hairy?" Jacob meant "heel catcher, trickster, con man, or scoundrel."[51] Neither of these names sounds very promising, but they were pretty accurate descriptions. Esau grew to be the manly, outdoorsy type of guy; and Jacob grew to be more of the nerdy, indoor type. When the Bible says Jacob was a mild man, the word actually means "whole" and "contented."[52] It gives the impression that he didn't feel the need to prove his skills as Esau seemed to do. This family's dysfunction is evident quite early. Isaac's favorite was Esau, but Rebekah's favorite was Jacob. This favoritism would lead to some problems!

What in the world is a birthright? In our culture, we think each child should get an equal portion of "the will," and we are upset if we think a sibling receives a bigger share than us. In this culture and family, the oldest male child received an extra portion—in this case, two-thirds of the estate—and was also expected to carry on the social and spiritual leadership of the family.[53] We can see that Esau didn't appreciate or respect his birthright, but Jacob did. Esau was caught up in his present needs and pleasures and was willing to give it all up for a bowl of soup in the moment. It's unlikely that this was just one bad decision that Esau made. Rather, Esau probably had developed a pattern of similar life choices. Esau had become the kind of guy who was willing to lose a third of his inheritance for some cheap lentil soup in the moment. He failed to see beyond his immediate circumstances.

God has given each of us a spiritual birthright full of abundant life, but so many of us don't bother to live in it. We spend more time Netflixing, scrolling, gaming, YouTubing, etc., than reading and meditating on God's Word. We are broken, and we know it. We suffer from so much anxiety, broken relationships, and low self-esteem. We don't come to the Life-Giver who tells us who we are, tells us to cast our cares on Him, and has the power to heal any broken heart. We can see that what Esau did was foolish, but we do the same thing every day. We trade the promises God gives us for a little something tasty in the moment.

Don't get me wrong. Many people pray, but their prayers are for themselves and their own prosperity. They aren't truly giving and receiving the breath of the Life-Giver. The presence of God changes us like it changed Abraham. It takes us out of our selfishness to a place where we forget about ourselves and live to give life to others. It takes away our fears and insecurities because we find our identity and are made whole by the one with the power to turn the desert into a garden.

REFLECTION QUESTIONS:

Where are your choices leading you? Are there areas in your own life that are simply focused in the moment, leading away from what you want or ought to be in the long run? Where has God been fitting in on your priority list recently?

_____

_____

_____

_____

_____

Think of some things you have been struggling with lately. Are any of them things the Bible has already promised victory over?

_____

_____

_____

_____

_____

GENESIS 26

The stage has been set between Esau and Jacob. Now, the narrative steps back to examine Isaac's character. Remember when there was a famine, and Abraham left to get food in Egypt? Now, we see Isaac doing the same thing, but God stopped him and told him not to leave. Isaac was not supposed to live anywhere except in the land that God had promised to him. God met with Isaac and let Isaac know that the covenant had not ended just because Abraham had died. God promised Isaac the land, the descendants, and the spiritual blessing. So Isaac had this awesome time with God and then ...

Remember when Abraham got scared and said his wife was his sister? Twice? Well, like father, like son. Isaac repeated his father's mistakes. While Abraham's statement was a half-truth, Isaac's was a complete lie. Keep in mind that the Abimelech Isaac met was not the same one with whom his father dealt. Abimelech is just a title like the word *king* or *prince*.[54] The ironic thing is that both Abraham and Isaac went to the same town and told the king the same lie. Coincidence? I think not. Even though God forgave Abraham, his sin still influenced his son to sin. Every time we sin, we do two things: we hurt our relationship with God, and we infect the world around us. Even when God forgives us, there is still an infection that spreads throughout our other relationships, and that disease has consequences.

Isn't it heartbreaking how Isaac was willing to trade his wife for the security that God had just promised him after God worked a miracle in bringing them together? This kind of betrayal has consequences on relationships. Isaac revealed to Rebekah that he was willing to betray her to get the security he wanted, and later, we see that Rebekah was willing to betray Isaac to get the security she wanted.

What we think is hidden is often obvious to others. Abimelech saw Isaac with Rebekah. Although the text is vague about what Abimelech saw, it was enough to convince him that they were not brother and sister! Once again, the "wicked" king acted more righteous than God's covenant man, and the "wicked" man tried to fix the wrong that Isaac had done. God used Abimelech to protect Isaac and Rebekah.

God blessed Isaac so greatly that his neighbors in Gerar became jealous and began sabotaging his wells. What was he doing living so close to them anyway? The neighbors don't want him there, so they shut off his water. Isaac moved and set up his tent in his neighbor's backyard. Rather than resist his neighbors, Isaac moved out of town only to find that they would still harass him. By the third move, the men of Gerar finally left him alone. Wells were needed to sustain life. Isaac went for the wells that sustained his father's life, thinking it would also sustain his life. God used the tension with the locals to get Isaac back toward Beersheba.

Just up the road in his father's old stomping ground, God

once again revealed Himself to Isaac and reiterated the covenant that He had made with Isaac's father. Again, God said, "I am the God your father served. I am the Life-Giver, and I am with you, so you have no reason to fear. I am going to continue my covenant with you and give you lots of descendants." Isaac's response was to build an altar—an act of repentance and worship. Isaac was letting God know that he would submit to God's definition of right and wrong, and God would be the one to sustain their lives.

There had been rumors of war between Isaac's people and Abimelech's people. Isaac had reason to be concerned, but after he surrendered, God worked out his relationship with his neighbors. Immediately afterward, Abimelech went to make peace with Isaac. Abimelech's people saw that God was with Isaac, so they went and asked Isaac to make a promise of peace because they were afraid of Isaac's God. Even though Abimelech hadn't treated him well, Isaac responded by giving and promoting peace. This response was in the image of the Life-Giver. When we let go and trust and worship God, He will take care of the details. On that same day, the wells burst forth with water, and Isaac allowed God to be his Sustainer.

The chapter closes with Esau, the manly man, all grown up and ready to have a wife. He didn't follow Grandpa Abraham's leadership, showing us again that he didn't appreciate the spiritual birthright he had. He chose to define good and evil how he wanted. Nor did Isaac seek out a wife for his son as his father, Abraham, had wisely done for him. Instead, Esau married not just one but two local Hittite women who didn't believe in Abraham's God and who would likely continue to lead Esau away from the Life-Giver. Isaac and Rebekah loved their baby, and it broke their hearts to see him choose wives who didn't reflect the image of God.

REFLECTION QUESTIONS:

Every family is dysfunctional in some way. Some are more dysfunctional than others, but we all need to reevaluate our ideas of a healthy family and learn from biblical principles. Are there patterns in your own life that you would or wouldn't want to be passed on to your children (or friends)? What patterns do you see yourself repeating from your own parents? What can you do to break the cycle and establish God-honoring practices in their place?

_____

_____

_____

_____

_____

Isaac represents the Life-Giver to Abimelech. What ideas about God do you think Abimelech got from Isaac? Do you think he got an accurate view?

_____

_____

_____

_____

We are often tempted to try to control and manipulate our circumstances to get what we want or think we need. Are there areas in your own life that you just need to turn over to God and trust Him with?

_____

_____

_____

_____

GENESIS 27

I f I (Ruth) had to describe this chapter in one word, it would be *ironic*. Jacob was plotting to steal what God had already promised him. He infected a lot of relationships with the disease of his sin, and then he spent most of his life trying to fix the mess he had made.

Isaac thought he was dying, so he decided that it was time to settle his affairs and make out his will. What should have been a sacred family affair became a series of manipulation games by everyone in the household. This scene would have made a theatrical reality TV show! Isaac secretly plotted to give his blessings to his older and favorite son, Esau. Isaac was a bit obsessed with Esau's manliness. He said he loved Esau's hunting, but he really couldn't even tell the difference between Esau's food and the sheep outside his tent. It wasn't the taste that he liked; he was proud of Esau and his hunting abilities. Isaac insisted on giving the blessing to Esau even though both God and Esau made it clear that Esau wasn't God's man. Isaac decided to do this secretly because he knew it wasn't right. In this house, they didn't trust one another—and with good reason!

Rebekah overheard Isaac's plan and decided to take action to secure her favorite son's future, so she told Jacob how to best trick her blind husband and steal what God had already promised. The end never justifies the means; God did not need Rebekah to help Him out. Later, we will see all kinds of relational consequences caused by this trickery and manipulation. Jacob didn't seem to have any moral problems with tricking and stealing, but he was concerned about the consequences of getting caught. When we decide to determine good and evil for ourselves, before long, our only concern becomes getting caught.

All four people in this scene were trying to deceive one another and God to manipulate the situation and get what they wanted. Remember that the consequences of the fall are a broken relationship with God and broken relationships with others. Here, we see everyone rebelling against God's plan and tearing apart their family relationships in the process.

The ironic thing is that the real blessing Isaac bestowed was God's promise to send them a deliverer who would transform them by taking the hell out of their hearts. They were stabbing one another to steal this blessing from God for themselves. Irony, so much irony. They were trying to use God like a lucky charm. Jacob not only lied to his father repeatedly, but he also did it in God's name. He said, "I am just following God's will." Nothing shuts down a conversation like that line. We often use that same line to keep others from questioning our actions and motivations. Isaac declared that Jacob, the deceiver, was now the spiritual leader of the home and inheritor of the promised property. This home was not off to a great start.

After Esau returned, Isaac and Esau realized they had been beaten. When Isaac planned this trick, he might have believed he was tricking God; but at that moment, Isaac realized God would not be tricked. Isaac admitted to Esau, "I tried to manipulate God, but He will not be manipulated. God has chosen, and there is nothing I can do about it."

Esau was devastated and cried for his father's blessing, but Esau didn't really want the true blessing of God's presence. He wanted a magical charm that would make him lucky and prosperous. He wanted to use God to achieve his own happiness. He cried, not because he was repentant but because he didn't succeed. He had already given his birthright away, but now he saw himself as a victim. Nothing builds the road to a miserable life quicker than thinking we are the victim. Once we get on this road and stop taking responsibility for our actions, we are doomed. Hebrews 12:15–17 warns us that if we become the victim in our own mind, we will never repent; we will destroy ourselves and everyone we touch.

Isaac did give Esau a "blessing" of sorts, but the best part of this blessing was that Esau would eventually become free of his victimhood, and this would free him from his brother's power over him. But for now, Jacob had power over Esau because Esau hated him. Esau's heart was creating hell as he plotted to kill Jacob in revenge.

To protect Jacob, Mama Rebekah convinced Isaac to send Jacob away under the guise of finding a suitable wife among her family back in Haran. This trip that was to last several weeks would turn into several decades. The mistrust and deception had torn apart their family because sin always destroys relationships. Rebekah had started out as a virtuous woman, but along the way, Isaac and Rebekah allowed their children and their own self-interest to come between them and damage their marriage. Their personal ambitions for their kids brought dysfunction to their relationship. Rebekah sort of won this battle, but God had already promised what she had manipulated to acquire for her son. In doing it her way, she was forced to send Jacob away, never to see him again. Everyone tried to win, and everyone ended up losing.

This story is a pretty good example of family dysfunction. They were all cruel to one another, but when we get really honest about our hearts, we realize we are much more like them than not, especially Esau. How often do we ask someone to pray for us to get what we want? How often do we pray to God to give us something we are craving? What we are really saying is "Give me your blessing so that I can have what I want." We want a lucky charm to guarantee our happiness and keep us from pain. The irony is that God has already given us His blessing to give us what our hearts truly desire, but with that comes the pain of complete surrender. We must surrender 100 percent of everything we hold dear; then, He will give us His life-giving spirit. This is the *real* blessing. He will take the hell out of our hearts and turn us into life-givers who breathe His goodness into others. We were made to reflect His image, and nothing brings real joy until we are also life-givers.

REFLECTION QUESTIONS

Imagine another ending to this account, one in which there was no deceit or manipulation. How might things have turned out differently had each surrendered to God and trusted Him to do what He had promised?

_____

_____

_____

_____

When someone wrongs us, our natural response is to hurt them back as much or usually a bit more than they hurt us. Do you struggle with the desire to get revenge? What is it that motivates us to do that?

_____

_____

_____

_____

_____

Have you ever prayed that God would give you something you wanted? Is this wrong? Jesus also prayed for something He wanted in the Garden of Gethsemane, but He ended with "Whatever happens, I want Your will above my own." What makes Jesus's prayer different than when we pray for what we want?

_____

_____

_____

_____

_____

GENESIS 28

saac realized that he couldn't manipulate God. He told Jacob to go get a wife from Rebekah's family who would honor Abraham's God. God had told Abraham that He was El Shaddai (God Almighty) in Genesis 17, and Isaac passed that truth down to Jacob. This God Almighty, creator and nourisher of life, will give you the land, the kids, and the blessing (ultimately Jesus) so that you will be a blessing to everyone else. Even after this dysfunctional family had played out their drama, God kept His promises. He wasn't doing it because Jacob was worthy but because God is faithful. Jacob, who had conned his brother and father out of the inheritance, went away for several decades, seemingly leaving without money, gifts, or possessions.

Esau discovered that the women of Canaan were breaking his parents' hearts. In an attempt to please his father, he sought out a third wife—this time, one of his cousins, a daughter of Ishmael. Later, we see that God did indeed bless Esau. It seems that Esau got off the victim road and took responsibility for his actions in the future.

Jacob went on the same long journey his mother had taken over seventy-five years before. This journey was an important season in his life, and the next few years would be pivotal. About three days into his journey, Jacob stopped for the night, went to sleep, and had a dream. In Jacob's dream, heaven and earth were overlapping, and Jacob realized that God was much closer and more involved in his life than he ever knew. Someday, this dream would become a reality when God would build a bridge between heaven and earth, and we would have a pathway into God's presence (see John 1:51). God spoke to Jacob for the first time and promised him all He had promised to Abraham and Isaac.

This moment was a life-changing experience. Jacob had heard about this God all his life, but suddenly, Jacob had encountered him personally. The covenant promise was his. God gave him an additional promise that God has also given to us in Philippians 1:6. A promise that God had started his work in Jacob, and God will stick with it. Then, He gave Jacob the best blessing of all. God promised His presence would be with him.

When Jacob woke up, he was mind-blown and declared this place was an amazing (sacred) place because God was there. He didn't seem to understand that the reason God was in this place was because Jacob was in this place. God had just promised to be with Jacob. Jacob set up a little memorial and called the place Bethel or "the house of God." Later, in Genesis 31, we see God come to Jacob and say, "Hey, remember me, you know, the God of Bethel?"

Ironically, Jacob is now bargaining with God for what God had just promised to give him. As if Jacob's offer of some money and a house was tempting to God. Jacob was unwilling to submit to God's deal; he wanted to make a deal on his own terms. "If you will be my lucky charm and give me what I want, then I will serve you. I will return to this place, make you a house, and give you one-tenth of all I make." God's vow was for God to bless everyone through Jacob. Jacob's vow was for everyone to bless Jacob through God. Not the same thing. God had promised to bless Jacob, and God knew that Jacob would never be happy until Jacob got rid of this selfishness. Welcome to the story of God chasing after Jacob.

REFLECTION QUESTIONS

Two wrongs don't make a right—and neither do three. While it was "culturally acceptable" for Esau to have several wives, this was never God's plan from the beginning. What are some ways we are tempted to make up for our mistakes by making another?

_____

_____

_____

_____

_____

Jacob tried to bargain with God, even though He had promised him so much. How do we try to bargain or manipulate God to do what we want? Have you ever tried to bargain with God? How did things work out for you? How can you tell if your prayers are manipulative?

_____

_____

_____

_____

_____

GENESIS 29

After running away from his dysfunctional family, Jacob started a dysfunctional family of his own. He arrived at a well near his uncle's house and immediately saw Rachel coming. Jacob went to find a wife and didn't waste any time. He nicely asked the other guys by the well to go away, but they informed him that they had gone to the well for water, and they weren't leaving until they got some. So when Jacob saw that Rachel (who apparently had no brothers) had also gone to water her sheep, he put on his charm and helped her.

Jacob got his game on and tried his pickup line. He greeted Rachel and cried loudly, telling her they were related. She had probably heard about her aunt Rebekah, so she brought him home to Daddy Laban. Remember him? Laban was very friendly with Jacob, especially when he discovered that Jacob would inherit a lot of money someday. After Jacob had stayed with them for about a month, Jacob requested that Rachel become his wife. As Jacob had arrived penniless without a dowry, Laban and Jacob made an agreement that Jacob would work for Laban for seven years in exchange for Rachel. While scholars disagree as to whether Leah's tender eyes were a positive or negative attribute,[55] Jacob found Rachel far more desirable than her older sister, Leah. Seven years was a long time (much longer than what would have been the cultural norm), but Jacob was in love, and it seems no price would have been too high. Seven years is a long time to wait, but if we really love someone, we are willing to wait for them.

After the seven years were up, the family celebrated with a big wedding. But to Jacob's astonishment, Laban cheated the cheater. The morning after the festivities, when Jacob was sober and could see clearly, he realized that he had been hoodwinked. Undoubtedly, Laban's daughters were in on the scheme, but it is tragic how Laban could do this not only to his nephew but to his daughters as well. Leah was now married to someone who didn't want her, and Rachel would now have to share her husband. Laban's greed was setting his daughters up for a lifetime of heartaches.

Interestingly, Laban actually repeated Jacob's own sin. When Jacob first went to Laban's house, he probably told Laban how he had tricked his father. Perhaps that was the seed that gave Laban his idea. Jacob tricked his father when he replaced the younger son with the older son, and now Laban tricked Jacob when he replaced the older daughter with the younger daughter. Even though God pardons our sins, He doesn't usually take away the consequences of our sins. After Jacob and Leah's honeymoon week was up, Jacob married Rachel. Then Jacob worked another seven years to pay for the second wife whom he loved the most. What a perfect setup for a dysfunctional family and intense sibling jealousy!

God saw Leah's pain and had compassion for her. This example illustrates how God can meet the needs of people in broken relationships. He is the El Shaddai and will be their Life-Giver and nurturer if they will crave Him. One of the things God did for Leah was comfort her in the form of many sons. The first three were named after the emotional pain she had endured because of the situation in which she found herself. Leah kept finding her identity and worth in what she could do and in how others perceived her instead of finding it in who God is. By the time she gave birth to her fourth son, there was a shift in her focus. This child's name was derived from the phrase "give thanks."[56] Note the difference: this was the first child she didn't name after her sorrow. At that moment, she was praising God and relying on Him to love and sustain her life.

REFLECTION QUESTIONS:

God had promised Leah that He would be her sustainer. Can God do that for someone who is stuck in a marriage today where they don't feel valued? How can God be their El Shaddai?

_____

_____

_____

_____

_____

Jacob ran seven hundred miles from home, yet his sins and deceit still caught up with him and backfired. Often, a new situation may distract us from our poor choices and character flaws, but it seldom fixes them. We just carry them into the next mess. What do we need to do to break the cycle?

_____

_____

_____

_____

_____

Stop and honestly evaluate your life here. Estimate how much time and energy you've spent on your appearance, performance, and image on social media in the last twenty-four hours; then compare that with how much time you've spent in God's presence and meditating on His words. Leah was finding her worth in her abilities and her public image. Like Leah, are you basing your worth on what you can do and in your public image, or are you basing your worth on your relationship with God? Basing our worth on anything other than our identity in Christ will lead to failure and heartache.

_____

_____

_____

_____

GENESIS 30

H ad social media been around during this time, imagine how this family would have been exploding their friends' feeds with all their drama! This chapter is just one pitiful episode after another. Jacob's obvious favoritism led his sister-wives to become jealous of each other and, in turn, play their man back and forth. Then they decided to get some other women involved since two weren't enough. The women were having lots of kids between the four of them and were even naming their kids after the competitive drama.

Oftentimes, when we are hurt, we get angry and blame others. For some reason, we feel more in control or justified when we blame others for our pain rather than acknowledge our insecurities and hurts. Here, we see Rachel was hurt that she couldn't have children, so she became angry and blamed her husband. Although Jacob recognized that it was God who had closed Rachel's womb, unlike his father, Isaac, the text never records that Jacob ever prayed for his wife. Jacob seems to be consumed with himself and his own schemes.

Rachel then had this great idea that her husband should sleep with yet another woman and have children on her behalf. (Basically, the same thing her grandmother-in-law Sarai had suggested to Abram. Remember how that turned out?) So Jacob used Bilhah like his grandpa had used Hagar. Rachel then took the baby and named him "to judge" or "vindicate."[57] She was so jealous of her sister that she saw this baby as God's revenge. Then, out of spite, Rachel insisted Bilhah have another child.

Leah seemed to have lost her focus on God and was caught up in the fight once again. She decided to play the same trick her sister had by adding yet another woman to the mix. Zilpah had a baby, and Leah named him "a troop comes!"[58] Apparently, by this time, it was an all-out war at home, and each new baby was just adding to the militia. Baby Asher arrived, and we see from his name that Leah cared more about what this baby would do for her happiness than the new life itself. Leah had several more children, and the war continued. Finally, after years of barrenness, God allowed Rachel to have a son. However, it was not enough, so she named him "He [God] will add"[59] (Joseph). All but one of these children were named after the war going on in this home. What a home to be born into!

Laban had many grandchildren through Jacob, all of whom were named after this family war that Laban had started. Jacob went to Laban and said he wanted to take his big dysfunctional family back home to Canaan. Laban knew God was blessing Laban through Jacob, so he wanted Jacob to stay close. The two made a business deal, and Jacob stayed.

Although Jacob was able to increase the fertility of his animals and grow a stellar flock, he couldn't help Rachel with her fertility problems. But considering the atmosphere in his home, he probably spent as much time in his fields as he could.

What is up with this weird system Jacob used to increase his flock? We often try to plot and scheme to increase our wealth or find the best bargain, but in the end, it is God who multiplies and provides. It's doubtful Jacob's superstitious methods did much, but we do know that God had promised to bless Jacob, and Jacob was blessed. In the next chapter, Jacob readily admitted that it was God who did the multiplying as Laban frequently changed the terms of the agreement. No matter what Jacob did with his flock, it would prosper because God said it would. Laban even knew that God blessed all that Jacob did and tried to manipulate the situation to his advantage. Once again, God honored his promise to Jacob even though Jacob didn't deserve it!

REFLECTION QUESTIONS:

Where is God mentioned in this chapter? What does that reveal about Jacob, Leah, and Rachel? How might things have been different had each called out to God?

_____

_____

_____

_____

_____

We often trust God in some areas; finances are a harder one. How often we try to scheme and save, neglect to be generous, invest in the market only to have the stock market crash, and find extra expenses at the end of the month. This does not mean we shouldn't save, but if we truly believed it was God who prospered our work and finances, how might our attitude change? How might our attitude toward giving change?

_____

_____

_____

_____

_____

GENESIS 31

N ot only was Jacob's home ripe for a drama-filled comedy show, but so was Laban's! Laban's sons had become jealous that Jacob had prospered so much, and Laban's daughters had grown bitter toward their father. The serpent had coaxed each family member to eat the fruit, causing pain, resentment, and heartache for everyone. Laban's sons reasoned that everything Jacob had, came from their father; therefore, Jacob was cheating them out of their inheritance. Notice that both Laban's and Jacob's possessions were increasing because of God's blessing, but Jacob's were growing faster. No matter how much God has blessed us, we can always see someone with more and feel sorry for ourselves. Laban was happy with what he had until he realized someone else had more.

God prepared Jacob to return to Canaan. First, God allowed Jacob's current situation to become uncomfortable. Then, He clearly spoke to Jacob in a dream. God said, "Jacob, remember Me, the God of Bethel? It is time to go back home." Laban might have tried to routinely cheat Jacob for his own advantage (and Jacob too had tried to manipulate the situation), but God revealed to Jacob that it was He who had caused Jacob to prosper. There was no way Jacob could have predicted how Laban would change his wages before the lambs were born. Jacob's flock was increasing because God was blessing him.

Jacob had a history of running away from his problems. Jacob saw it as a good move to try again. He told his wives his secret plan. He was going to make a run for it while Laban and the other shepherds were busy shearing sheep. For the first and only time, we see Rachel and Leah agreeing together. What could unite two enemies after years of feuding? A common enemy. Both of them likely still felt used and cheated by their father. They were united and were plotting with their husband. God had already told Jacob that he would have a safe journey, but Jacob snuck off because he didn't trust God to protect him.

We don't know why she did it, but Rachel stole her father's idols. Some have speculated that it was an act of revenge or that the idols represented an inheritance right, a type of land deed;[60] or more likely, Rachel did not want her father to be able to follow them through divination. Rachel's later treatment of the idols indicated she certainly didn't respect them.

Three days after they left, Laban found out, and he was mad! When he caught up to them, God warned him in a dream to beware of what he would do with Jacob because Jacob was under God's protection. This warning implies that Laban had some bad intentions. Jacob's family and livestock had traveled well over three hundred miles in ten days, and Laban wasn't going to let him go without a confrontation. He accused Jacob of taking his daughters hostage. He also pretended he wanted to celebrate Jacob's departure, but no one bought it. Then he threatened Jacob and said the only thing stopping him from harming him was

Jacob's God. Just when we thought Laban might let the matter rest, he accused Jacob of stealing his idols. Can I just say it is pretty pathetic to worship a god that you have to protect because they can't protect themselves?

Jacob admitted that he didn't trust his own God to protect him and his family from Laban. Then Jacob told Laban that he might kill anyone that Laban found with the idols. Tragically, Rachel, the person Jacob felt closest to, continued the family pattern of deception. It is also tragic that Laban went after his own daughters with the belief that he would find the idols and possibly kill one of them. Rachel successfully deceived her father by hiding them in her seat with the excuse she's on her period.

Laban returned to Jacob without his idols or any other stolen property. Now, it was Jacob's turn to shame Laban, and he had it out with him. Jacob had a major meltdown and laid out all his frustration with Laban from day one. You know this speech has been going over and over in his mind for a long time. At the end of his speech, he gave God credit for blessing him despite Laban's trickery. Interestingly, Jacob had yet to claim God as his own. He said this was the God of Abraham and Isaac, but he didn't list himself—yet.

Then, Laban responded, "Everything you have is actually mine, but since I'm a nice guy, you can have it." We all know that Laban was known for his generosity. Keep in mind that all these people that Laban was claiming as his own wanted to leave Laban. Then, Laban suggested they make a covenant before God. By doing this, Laban was no longer treating Jacob as a clan member under his jurisdiction but as an equal. What Laban said might sound sweet on the surface, but he was really saying, "If you hurt my daughters or take other wives, may God punish you, and if you cross this line we're making, I won't be so nice next time." Laban was not setting things up well for happy family reunions! So then, they had a campout, roasted hamburgers, and spent the night celebrating their agreement. The next morning, Laban got up, said sweet goodbyes, and left; and we never heard from him again.

How tragic that Laban broke with his family because he threatened their father with death if he ever returned. In his anger and selfishness, Laban was trying to punish them; but instead, he just isolated and punished himself. Now, his family is happily free of him. As you look through this book, notice how every time we sin against God, we also damage our relationships with one another. Similarly, when we are in the right relationship with God, we reflect the Life-Giver, and our relationships with others often prosper.

REFLECTION QUESTIONS:

God used a couple of different ways to communicate His will that Jacob return to Canaan. In what ways does God communicate His will to us today?

_____

_____

_____

_____

Look at the mess that Jacob made when he left Laban. He chose to sneak off because he was afraid of Laban, even after God had promised to bring him home safely. What if Jacob had asked God how to leave Laban? How do you think he could have been a better witness of God's character to everyone involved?

_____

_____

When Laban caught up with them, He said he intended to hurt them, but God told him not to. Laban was going to hurt his own kids and grandkids. Sin often leads us to hurt or destroy our own families. Laban drew a line that neither was to cross, so now, he would never see his family again. Talk about shooting himself in the foot. How could he have done that differently? Have you ever separated yourself from family or friends because of your own pride or selfishness?

GENESIS 32

Jacob was on the borders of Canaan, and he saw the angels of God. He realized that there was an entire camp of angels around him! If God be for him, who could stand against him, right? Knowing that God was in this place, Jacob decided this was where he wanted to meet his brother. He sent messengers on a several-day journey to his brother in the land of Edom, saying, "I am your servant. I've been working with Uncle Laban, and now, I have lots of stuff. So don't worry. I am not after your stuff. I know I don't deserve it, but please don't be angry with me. Sincerely yours, Brother Jacob." After waiting in great anticipation, Jacob's messengers returned and told him that Esau was bringing 400 men with him! (Remember how Grandpa Abraham defeated five kings and their armies with only 318 men? This situation is not looking good!)

Jacob's mother had promised to send for Jacob when Esau had

gotten over him, but Rebekah never had, so it was reasonable to assume that Esau was still bitter. Jacob had burned his bridges behind him with Laban, and Esau and his men were in front of him. Jacob found himself trapped between two men who had sworn to kill him. Even though he had just seen an army of God's angels, Jacob really started losing it. Rather than trust God in this seemingly impossible situation, he did what Jacob did best and started planning his tricks. He forgot about the camp of angels guarding him and split all his people and stuff into two camps of his own. He thought that if Esau were to slaughter one group, the other could escape.

For the first time in the recorded life of Jacob, Jacob called on God. Notice that it was only when he felt completely trapped that he turned to God. Although he prayed to God, he still didn't call Him "my God" but the God of Dad and Grandpa. Jacob was finally talking to God with humility and praise. His first discussion with God at Bethel was full of pride and entitlement, but in this case, his prayer was a plea for God to deliver him. He also admitted that he wasn't worthy but was asking because he knew God was good. Even though Jacob said a sweet prayer, he still didn't trust God to deliver him. When God didn't give him a sign of protection, Jacob started scheming again.

Here, the self-centered nature of Jacob comes into full view. First, he separated 550 animals into three groups to send ahead as appeasement gifts to Esau, followed by his wives and kids, but he stayed behind. He was willing to give up everything and everyone except himself. If need be, He was willing to sacrifice all their lives to protect his own. That night, Jacob was alone on one side of the river, and a mysterious man started to wrestle with him. We soon discover that this was no ordinary man but God in the form of a man. What Jacob has been doing all his life played out physically in a wrestling match. Jacob had been growing hell in his heart and had hurt everyone with whom he had come into contact. Now, God had come to wrestle him over it.

Jacob couldn't humble himself to admit he had a problem. Jacob's pride and selfishness were fighting back, but God had come to change him into the man God had created him to be. However, Jacob wouldn't surrender himself to God. He wanted to be his own boss and rule his own life. He was willing to sacrifice his things, his animals, his wives, and even his children but not himself. In the darkness, God and Jacob wrestled all night. Certainly, God could have easily overpowered Jacob at any time, but God doesn't overpower our will. He painstakingly and patiently wrestles with us and allows us to make our own choices. He wanted Jacob to choose to surrender and trust Him no matter the outcome with Esau.

Jacob probably thought it was going well until the moment God put Jacob's hip out of the socket, yet Jacob still didn't give up. God then asked Jacob his name. Did God not know with whom He was wrestling? In the Bible, names have deep meanings that often reflect a person's character. God was asking Jacob to confess his broken character. God told him that He wanted Jacob to stop being a deceiver and heal grasper. While it seems Jacob never truly came to the end of himself and never fully enjoyed all God had for him, he was a changed man through the experience. Jacob had been fighting enemies all his life without ever realizing his biggest enemy was himself.

Jacob made a memorial to commemorate the event by naming the place Peniel, meaning "face of God."[61] God also made a memorial for Jacob that day. For the rest of his life, Jacob would walk with a limp, reminding him of the night he wrestled with God. One of the best gifts God can give us is that He doesn't give up, but He keeps on coming after us and wrestling with us to free us from the hell growing in our hearts.

REFLECTION QUESTIONS:

Why is it that a crisis often causes us to call out to God? How have you seen God use crises in your own life to bring you closer to Him?

The enemy often tells us that God can't be trusted, but trusting Him is the only way to find true freedom! Like Jacob, is there anything you're wrestling with God over that you can't seem to surrender to Him?

Jacob's name was a constant reminder of his broken past as a deceiver and trickster. In giving Jacob a new name, God wanted Jacob's life to head in a different direction. When we have had a life-changing moment with God, it is important that we do something that will help us remember it. Some people like to journal their experiences, others take real stones and write on them, and some people make something that hangs on their walls.

What can you do so that you don't forget those pivotal times when
God met with and changed you?

_____

_____

_____

_____

_____

GENESIS 33

The next day, Jacob saw his brother coming with his four hundred men. The tension was high. Was Esau still holding a grudge? Had the gifts calmed Esau's anger? What kind of punishment might Esau have in mind, with four hundred men as backup? Jacob took a deep breath and lined up his family in order of their importance to him. (Yes, we already know this is a dysfunctional family.) But we now begin to see a change in Jacob. The day before, he was putting everyone in front of himself; but here, Jacob went out in front to face his accuser. In fear and nervousness, Jacob bowed to the ground before Esau, demonstrating to his brother that he had no desire to "rule over him" as their father's blessing had stated he would.

The manly hunter who had sworn to kill Jacob went running toward him. We have had days that didn't go quite like we expected, and this was Jacob's "you won't believe what just happened" moment. He expected to be murdered but instead experienced a joyous reunion. Esau's charge turned into an open embrace of hugs and tears. It was obvious that God had been working not only on Jacob but on Esau too. How often do we assume the worst and stress out rather than surrender the circumstances and trust God? Jacob (probably still in shock) nicely introduced his family to the brother that he thought would murder them all.

When Esau and Jacob separated all those years ago, they fought because neither one felt they had enough blessings. When they met again, they both said, "I have enough." God had abundantly blessed both Jacob and Esau, but Jacob needed Esau to take the gifts of livestock because it was Jacob's way of apologizing, and it was Esau's way of saying he forgave him. The giving and accepting of these gifts was a sign of friendship and restoration between them.

Unfortunately, Jacob hadn't embraced his new identity as Israel and still didn't seem to trust God or his brother. After Esau invited Jacob to join him in Edom, Jacob made an excuse to wait a few days before promising that he would travel behind Esau. However, the deceiver came out again, and Jacob traveled in the opposite direction. Jacob went just across the Jabbok River to Succoth. Just as Jacob was on the fence spiritually with God, he settled on the edge of Canaan, not yet crossing the Jordan to the Promised Land.

Between verses 17 and 18, it seems several years passed before Jacob and his family finally crossed the Jordan and entered Canaan, ending up in Shechem. Here, just outside Shechem, Jacob bought some land, set up camp, and built an altar to God. This is the first time in the recorded life of Jacob that he built an altar to God. Why do people build altars? To sacrifice. Why do people sacrifice? To demonstrate their need for a Savior. Jacob called the altar "God, the God of Israel." For the first time, Jacob began to accept the name and identity God gave him. This was also the first time Jacob called out to God as "my God." Every time Jacob spoke of God previously, it was always "the God of my father, Isaac," and "the God of Grandfather Abraham." Jacob seemed to be making some spiritual progress, but it would be a while before he really began to accept his new identity in God. Unfortunately, Jacob would keep wrestling back and forth between "deceiver" and "God struggler" for the rest of his life. This pattern seems to follow his choices and actions. There are times when Jacob looks like he is a surrendered man, but then, we see him deceiving others again. I truly believe the Life-Giver wanted to do something deeper in Jacob's life, but Jacob struggled with surrendering to God and learning to live and walk in His presence. If only there were a way to take the hell out of Jacob's heart! If only the problem could be fixed rather than just covered by God's mercy. This problem is one that God will continue to wrestle with His people over for centuries to come until the Life-Giver comes in the flesh. He comes as the serpent crusher not only to take the guilt of our sins away but also to take away the disease that makes us want to hurt others in the first place.

Jesus came and brought His kingdom to earth. How awesome that you and I are living in these days. We can surrender to the Life-Giver and have Him transform us to the core. What is living inside of us is our own worst enemy, and He came to completely take it out. Anything that is keeping us from giving ourselves to Him completely is just the snake whispering in our ears. The snake hates every part of you and wants to see your life destroyed. Allow the One who made you to breathe His life into you again until you are completely alive in Him.

REFLECTION QUESTIONS:

How often we worry, stress, and strategize over things that never happen. Jacob was convinced Esau's four hundred men were out to slaughter him, but it turned out to be a welcoming committee! How does our view of God affect our worries and anxieties?

_____

_____

_____

_____

In the last chapter, Jacob had seen an entire army of angels camping around him. Why do you think he was still so afraid of Esau?

_____

_____

_____

_____

Jacob had wrestled with God all night. Why didn't God give up? What does this say about God? Why didn't Jacob give up? What is God wrestling with you about today? What is the snake telling you about who God is and who you are?

_____

_____

_____

_____

GENESIS 34

Most people who write books about their ancestors or their founding fathers paint them in the best possible light. The Bible is very different. The Bible includes the good, the bad, and the ugly. This chapter is an awful story of some awful people, but remember, the Bible isn't a story about good people. It is a story about a good God.

Jacob and his family have purchased land and set up camp on the outskirts of the city of Shechem. Dinah, Leah's daughter, started hanging out with the other young ladies of Shechem. Before long, she caught the attention of a man named Shechem, who began to lust after her and raped her. The man told his dad (who happened to be the city's ruler) that he must marry her. Jacob heard about it and waited without doing anything until her brothers came home. Keep in mind that during this time, there was no police force or justice system. It was up to individuals to make sure justice was done. The brothers were justifiably angry at Shechem and upset that their father hadn't done anything about the situation. Perhaps the sons feel that Jacob would have responded differently had this happened to a daughter of Rachel.

When Hamor, Shechem's dad, arrived to talk to Jacob, Hamor didn't apologize or even acknowledge that his son did anything wrong toward Dinah. He just asked Jacob for Dinah and suggested an alliance between the city and Jacob's family. He proposed that they intermarry, exchange wives, and mix their families. Hamor also suggested that they could trade and help each other economically. When Hamor told them to "dwell with us," he was saying, "Let's be partners."

This decision wasn't just about Shechem and Dinah; they were establishing a pattern for what was acceptable with the future nation of Israel. God did not want them to marry the Canaanites because the Canaanites didn't accept God's definition of right and wrong. At this point, Shechem hijacked the conversation and passionately asked Jacob to simply name his price.

Jacob was strangely silent on the matter and allowed Simeon and Levi (also sons of Leah) and his other sons to make the negotiations. They had repeatedly seen their dad and uncle scheme to trick people. Jacob's sons agreed to the alliance and intermarriage if all the men of Shechem would be circumcised. The brothers used what was to be a symbol of God's life-giving covenant to become a means of death and destruction for this community. They used their "religious convictions" to convince Hamor and Shechem of their sincerity. Hamor and Shechem bought it and said, "Deal."

How in the world did the men of Shechem agree to this? The text notes that Shechem was the most honorable (or important) member of his family. This description doesn't mean he was morally superior but signifies that Shechem had influence and was obviously used to getting what he wanted. Hamor and Shechem managed to persuade the men of the whole city to be circumcised for this deal they made. The men of Shechem saw dollar signs and liked the idea of being partners with this big rich family.

Three days after the procedure (no anesthetics in this era), while the men were still in considerable pain, Simeon and Levi rescued Dinah from Shechem's home. They took their revenge not just on Prince Shechem but on the whole city of Shechem. They slaughtered every male in the city! If that wasn't enough, the other brothers also helped to loot their possessions and capture the women and children!

Jacob's sons justified their actions by what Shechem did to their sister, but they took revenge on the whole group of people, not just the inflictor. When we have been hurt and don't surrender it to God, that hurt grows in our hearts till we desire more than justice; we desire revenge. Revenge is never satisfied until the hurt we inflict on others is greater than the hurt they inflicted on us.

Do you remember why God commanded Abraham's descendants to be circumcised? It was a symbol but not a status symbol. The process was gross and painful, but the hell they were growing inside of them was also gross and painful. God wanted them to understand that they were born with something in their hearts that needed to be taken out if they wanted to really be alive. This act was to be a sign to them and everyone else that they belonged to the God of Abraham. It was a statement of faith that one day, God would also circumcise their hearts and take the hell out of them. The whole point of circumcision was acknowledging the sin and selfishness problem, but now, we have a bunch of pagan men who got circumcised in the hope of getting wealthy. Then Jacob's sons grow hell in their hearts to literally stab and murder all the men of Shechem. Jacob's sons took all the wealth, possessions, women, and children. Rather than spreading the Life-Giver and being a blessing as God had intended, Jacob's sons spread the infection from their souls like a plague to everyone they touched. The people who were supposed to reflect the Life-Giver had slaughtered a whole city.

Jacob's response to the fiasco was equally pathetic. He wasn't concerned so much with his sons' actions as he was about his own safety. Jacob blamed his sons for repeating his character flaws. They grew up in the home of the deceiver who would use God for his own gain. They followed the blueprint he laid out for them, but the same song, second verse, is always a little bit louder and a little bit worse.

Let's recap. God appeared to Abraham for the purpose of developing him and his family to reflect His character and bless the world. In Genesis 18, God said, "For I have known him [Abraham], in order that he may command his children and his household after him, that they keep the way of the Lord, to do righteousness and justice, that the Lord may bring to Abraham what He has spoken to him." We're only four generations in, and God is trying to develop this family into a nation that would represent Him; but so far, things are not off to a good start. What is it going to take for God to mold this family to accomplish His life-giving purpose? What's it going to take to turn the family of Jacob into the family of Israel?

REFLECTION QUESTIONS:

What were some of the shortcomings of Abraham? What about Isaac? Jacob? And now his sons? What patterns do you see?

_____

_____

_____

_____

_____

Take a moment and reflect on your own family. What positive and negative patterns do you see in your own life? What can you do (with the help of the Spirit) to overcome these unhealthy or sinful patterns so that they are not passed onto your own children or grandchildren?

_____

_____

_____

_____

_____

Anytime humans want justice, we often aren't satisfied until we actually have revenge. Without God's transformation, the oppressed always become the oppressor when given the opportunity. Think of something you want justice for in the world. How can we promote justice without hurting the innocent?

_____

_____

_____

_____

GENESIS 35

After the mess in the last chapter, God spoke to Jacob, "Remember me? Apparently not. I am the God from Bethel. Now go back there to live, build an altar, and let's talk." Before the family made the twenty-mile trek southward, Jacob told his family to prepare themselves by disposing of their idols, purifying themselves, and changing their clothes. While this family was supposed to be God's covenant family, we know Rachel had stolen her father's idols. Now, his sons seem to have picked up some along the way too, perhaps in the loot they had taken from Shechem. Whether or not they had worshipped them, sin was crouching at their door. Jacob was encouraging them to do outwardly what they needed to be doing inwardly. Changing their clothes and cleaning themselves is a symbolic way to express their need to get rid of their wicked ways and humble themselves before God. While the world may stain us on the outside, the bigger problem is that something filthy from the inside keeps leaking out of us.

While Jacob had good reason to be concerned about retribution from the other Canaanite cities, God was already at work to protect this undeserving family by causing the surrounding towns to fear Jacob's family. While the Bible never mentions the death of Jacob's mother, Rebekah, we are told that Rebekah's nurse, Deborah, died while Jacob was near Bethel. Rebekah likely died while Jacob was in Haran. Had Deborah come to Haran to bring Jacob the news? Had she only recently come to find Jacob to give him news of his ailing father? We're simply not told. From the name that Jacob called the site of her burial, "Terebinth of Weeping," we get the hint that Jacob was deeply grieved at her passing. We know Jacob spent a lot of time around the tents as a child. Perhaps she had been like a second mother to Jacob in his youth.

Afterward, God showed up again and spoke to Jacob. Why did God keep appearing to Jacob and telling him the same thing? When a parent keeps repeating themselves, it is usually because the child isn't getting it. God's repetition tells us that the snake had Jacob on speed dial and was asking him those same questions, "Is God really who He says He is? Are you really who God says you are?" Notice every time God spoke to him, He repeated these same three things: (1) God told him who God was, (2) God told him who Jacob was, and (3) God told him the promise.

Remember when God changed Jacob's name to Israel? Other than using it in naming the altar at Shechem, Jacob continued to identify himself as a "deceiver" instead of a "God wrestler." God wanted Jacob to stop being the deceiver and start living for the God who had invested so much in Jacob. Here, God told him a second time, "Israel is now your name." God once again blessed him and reminded him of the covenant He had made first with Grandpa Abraham, with Daddy Isaac, and then with Jacob or Israel. God had chosen Jacob and his family to be the agents through whom all nations would be blessed. In response, Jacob built a memorial and worshipped God.

The family packed up camp and began moving farther southward. Leaving Bethel, they paused near Ephrath (Bethlehem), where Rachel went into difficult labor. Rachel had a second son, but she died in childbirth. Just before she died, she named the child "son of my sorrow"; but Jacob refused to be reminded of his wife's death every time he called his son, so he changed his name to "son of my right hand," signifying Jacob's favor toward the child. After erecting a memorial stone for his wife, for the first time, Jacob took on the name Israel. Tragedy often drives us closer to God.

The family moved on from Ephrath to Migdal Eder. Here, we have a brief account of Reuben, Jacob's firstborn son of Leah, sleeping with his father's concubine Bilhah. What? There is far more going on here than unrestrained sexual passion. Rachel had used Bilhah to try to hurt Leah when Reuben was a little boy. Reuben might have been trying to take revenge for his mother's pain. From a cultural standpoint, Reuben was also making a bold move to lay claim as the family's new patriarch. Having sex with a leader or king's concubines was a power play to usurp their authority. As we have come to expect of Jacob, he did nothing about it at the time. However, on his deathbed, Jacob will call down a curse on Reuben for this power play. Now, the oldest three sons have sinned grievously. Would Jacob's other sons be any better? The next few verses give a list of the twelve sons of Jacob. What we have learned about them so far is not too impressive, but God has still chosen to work with and through them. God has got His work cut out for Him in developing this family into a nation that will reflect His life-giving character to the world!

The chapter closes with Jacob and Esau at the old homestead in Hebron, standing by the deathbed of their father, Isaac. The scene is similar to Isaac and Ishmael at Abraham's passing, but somehow, we just don't feel as optimistic about the direction this family is going. Isaac was 180 years old and had the opportunity to meet all of Jacob's descendants. Isaac died, and his sons worked together to bury him in the same cave as their grandfather, Abraham.

In the middle of this chapter, God told Jacob to start going by the name of Israel; but it wasn't until he buried his wife, Rachel, that he took on the name personally for the first time. He stayed Israel for a while, but by the time he visited his father's house, he was back to Jacob. As you read the next few chapters, notice how he goes back and forth from Jacob to Israel. His choices also go back and forth: good choices and bad choices.

REFLECTION QUESTIONS:

We don't generally think of having idols today, but idols were a way to try to use god or gods to get what they wanted. When it comes down to it, they were just worshipping themselves and doing something that they hoped would help them get what they wanted. In what ways do we do that today?

_____

_____

_____

_____

_____

Jacob flipped between the names Jacob and Israel for the rest of his life. What old habits do you keep falling back into that steal your spiritual victory? Anytime we want to break a pattern, we need three things: (1) surrender to God, (2) accountability, and

(3) boundaries that we set up to protect ourselves. Today, make a plan to meet with someone with whom you can be accountable. Make sure the person isn't someone who is also struggling with the same thing but someone who has victory in this area. (1) Ask them to pray with you as you surrender it to God. (2) Ask them to keep you accountable with times and dates to meet. (3) Ask them to help you set boundaries for yourself. (4) Make a physical memorial to remind you of this day, such as a rock or something for your wall. This is the day you surrendered it to God, and you need to always remember this victory!

GENESIS 36

H ere, Esau has a whole chapter dedicated to him and his descendants. The first two wives of Esau were from Canaan. Remember how Rebekah and Isaac were brokenhearted over the wives that Esau chose? The wives had beliefs and made choices that were contrary to the God of Abraham and Isaac. Then, Esau decided to get a third wife, this time from Ishmael's family, in an attempt to please his parents. From these three wives, Esau had five sons.

The last time Esau and Jacob were together in the presence of their father, they couldn't live together because they were fighting over stuff neither of them had yet. Each of them feared they wouldn't get enough when Daddy died, but God had blessed each of them. In fact, now, they can't live together because they have too much stuff. How ironic! Most of their possessions were animals. Living in a dry region with only about eight to twelve inches of rain each year, they needed more land to support their animals. Similar to the separation of Abraham and Lot, Jacob stayed near the family homestead, and Esau packed up and went southwest to Mount Seir. This land became known as Edom in honor of Esau.

Esau's family became known as the Edomites, so Esau was also the father of a big nation. Esau's descendants will be mentioned in the Bible over one hundred times. Later, when Israel's descendants were headed to the Promised Land, Esau's descendants wouldn't let them go through Edom. However, even though they made life difficult for the Israelites, in Deuteronomy, God told them to respect the Edomites because "he is your brother."[62] God saw the big picture and reminded these two nations that they were still family many years later. The nations of Edom and Israel have this long-term love-hate relationship.

Although reading through a list of names seems a bit boring to our ears, chapters such as these help connect people, places, promises, and accounts. Besides Edom, one of the main names we should watch for on this list is Amalek, who would become the father of the Amalekites. This chapter tells us that the Amalekites were actually descendants of Esau and some of his in-laws. These people would become long-term enemies of Israel when the Israelites returned to the Promised Land. As we reflect on this chapter, the most obvious lesson is that God keeps his promises. Even though Esau did not receive "the blessing," God still blessed him with possessions, land, children, nations, and kings.

REFLECTION QUESTIONS:

It is sobering that Esau and Jacob couldn't live together because of jealousy over stuff they didn't even have yet. Then later, they couldn't live together because they had too much stuff. Often, the love of things breaks relationships. How have you seen it break relationships in your own family or friendships?

_____

_____

_____

_____

_____

Both Esau and Jacob chose to have more than one wife. In both situations, we see that it caused problems in other relationships. Although we may not be marrying more than one person at a time, unfaithfulness in marriage is no stranger in American culture. What are some ways we show unfaithfulness to our spouse? How do these choices cause problems in relationships with others who aren't in the marriages, such as children, parents, etc.?

_____

_____

_____

_____

_____

GENESIS 37

The story of Joseph is beyond remarkable. It is mind-blowing. He suffered more than most of us ever will and triumphed more than most of us would ever dream. Through it all, we never see him complain or compromise his faith.

Jacob's children were born into a seriously dysfunctional family. Remember how most of them were named for the fight that was going on in their home? My favorite name was Gad, meaning "behold, a troop cometh."[63] Nothing says "war in the home" like naming your children after militia. So these boys were born into conflict, and in conflict, they remained. We are all somewhat dysfunctional. We come from dysfunctional families and then start dysfunctional relationships all of our own, but God can still work in imperfect people. He's had lots of practice taking impossible situations and making something good out of it.

The first scene of this story of Joseph's life opens when Joseph is seventeen years old. He was with his older brothers in the field, and he came home to Dad and reported that they weren't doing their jobs. Nothing irritates a sibling more than a tattletale. Just as Jacob's parents had played favorites, Jacob repeated the same parenting style with Joseph as his favorite. Jacob didn't even try to hide it but poured on the gifts and attention. The brothers grew more jealous and resentful with each passing day to the point they couldn't talk to him without having conflict!

If you think you've had a rough childhood, put yourself in Joseph's shoes for a moment: Joseph grew up with ten older brothers, two of whom murdered a village; the oldest slept with his stepmom; his older sister had been raped and would probably never marry; and his dad and grandpa Laban weren't on speaking terms. His other grandfather and his biological mother died, leaving him with three stepmothers, at least two of whom were bitter toward his mom. He was his father's favorite, but this made the rest of the family mad at him. If this had happened in today's society, this kid would have been in counseling for the rest of his life!

Joseph didn't help things when he told his brothers about one of his dreams. This dream had everyone else's grain bowing down to his grain, implying that someday, his brothers would submit to him. No older sibling wants to hear their little brother bragging about being their boss. As if things weren't bad enough, Joseph told them a second dream where not only his brothers but even Mom and Dad worshipped Joseph! Now, Dad even thought Joseph was carrying this a bit too far. Some things may be best left unsaid.

Jacob sent Joseph off again to check up on his brothers some fifty miles away, caring for the sheep around Shechem. (Remember, this is the place where they had murdered and looted in revenge for their sister.) When Joseph arrived, his brothers were nowhere to be found, but Joseph just so happened to encounter a man who just so happened to overhear where his brothers were heading. After traveling another twenty miles northward, he spotted them near Dothan.

The brothers saw him coming and decided they were done. They weren't putting up with this little snitch anymore. The serpent whispered to them, and the hell in their hearts grew until they decided to kill him. This is *huge!* They were already plotting how to cover it up, knowing full well their father would be devastated. Reuben, the oldest brother, wanted to save Joseph for his dad's sake. While this is a positive move on Reuben's part, he was supposed to be the leader. It would have been a lot better if Reuben had stood up to his brothers. Instead, he tried to trick them, but he got tricked instead. See a pattern here? He had lost his window of opportunity and would live with regret for decades to come.

The brothers threw him into a pit and ate a meal while Joseph screamed for them to let him out. This is sick; they enjoyed their meal and listened to him scream while they plotted to kill him. His screams and cries would haunt them for decades (Genesis 42:21). It just so happened that at this opportune time, a caravan of Ishmaelite and Midianite traders passed in the distance. Judah then decided they wanted more from Joseph than just his death; they wanted a profit. While Reuben was away, the other brothers sold Joseph as a slave to the passing traders. Note the irony: Ishmael's mother was a slave to Isaac's mother, and now, Ishmael's descendants were buying and trading one of Isaac's descendants as a slave. Joseph was on his way to Egypt with his brothers, thinking they had defeated Joseph's dreams, but they actually just put them into action.

Reuben was grieved when he realized what his brothers had done. To hide their actions from their dad, they killed one of the goats and covered Joseph's coat with blood. Then they took the coat to Jacob and told him that they just found it like that. This ploy was a pretty heartless way to deceive their dad, but they had learned deception from the master himself. Then, they all tried to comfort him. What? Yes. Yes. They all tried to comfort him. Once again, notice the Jacob-Israel name change. He began this chapter as Israel, but after this tragedy of believing his beloved son to have been devoured by wild animals, his name immediately switched back to Jacob. Jacob might have blamed himself for his son's demise. After all, it was Jacob who had asked his teenage son to make the fifty-plus-mile journey to Shechem. Jacob's misery would mark him for the rest of his life.

The chapter ends with Joseph arriving in Egypt, and it just so happens that Joseph was sold as a slave to a high-ranking military officer. Joseph was 250 miles from home, and the only person who seemed to love him thought he was dead. Why would God allow this to happen to Joseph? Surely, it would have been Simeon or Levi who would deserve the life of a slave! But seventeen-year-old Joseph? He's not even a legal adult by American standards!

REFLECTION QUESTIONS:

God isn't mentioned in this chapter. In fact, it looks like He is absent, but is He? Throughout the chapter, we see a series of coincidences. Later, we see how all these pieces work together to accomplish a greater purpose. How have you seen God use "it just so happened" moments in your own life to accomplish a greater purpose? Can you look back on a time in your life when it had looked like God was absent, but now you see how He led through the whole thing? Is there an area in your life now that He seems absent?

_____

_____

Joseph was from a seriously dysfunctional family! Are there parts of Joseph's family with which you can identify? How does God accomplishing His purpose in Joseph's life give you hope?

_____

_____

_____

_____

_____

GENESIS 38

What happened to Joseph? Why are we talking about Judah now? This whole chapter almost feels out of place, but it does provide a contrast for the choices Joseph will make. It will also provide some insights into Judah's choices later in the book. Judah was the fourth son of Leah and the next in line to inherit the promised blessing because the first three blew it. By now, we should know that God seldom chooses who we would expect to accomplish his plans. We don't find out till the end of the book which son inherited the promise, but spoiler alert, it's Judah. Reuben had slept with his father's concubine, and Simeon and Levi slaughtered the city of Shechem. All we have heard about Judah so far is that he was the one to suggest they sell Joseph because killing him wouldn't profit them any.

By now, we know marrying the local population is not a good

idea, but Judah married a Canaanite woman. They had three sons: Er, Onan, and Shelah. Judah also found Er a Canaanite wife named Tamar, but God killed Er because he was so wicked. We don't know what his wicked sins were, but they had to have been pretty bad because this family definitely isn't spotless! Now, young Tamar was left a widow without children. In this period, before Social Security or welfare, widows had no means of support and (usually) no inheritance. Their only means of support was to rely on their male children to provide for them. If a woman became a widow before having children, it was customary for one of the husband's brothers to give her a child who would be considered the dead man's heir. This sounds superstrange to us, but keep in mind this was also an era of arranged marriages. Now, Judah's second son, Onan, was supposed to give Tamar a child. He had sex with her but wouldn't let her get pregnant. God was angry with Onan for tricking Tamar and using her as a sex object with no intention of providing for her needs, so God killed Onan also.

Judah promised Tamar that if she went back to live with her family, she could marry Shelah when he was old enough. Tamar complied, but when Shelah grew up, Judah broke his promise. Tamar was stuck because, in their culture, she was pledged to Shelah and couldn't do anything without Judah's approval. Her future and Judah's line were in jeopardy. After Judah's wife died, Tamar heard that Judah was going on a business trip and devised a plan. She put on the clothes of a shrine prostitute, which included a veil over her face, intending to seduce her father-in-law. The Canaanites believed in having sex with cult prostitutes as worship to the local gods. This act was believed to be pleasing to the local gods, who, in turn, would bring fertility and rain to their fields. However, these degrading acts were condemned by the Life-Giver. Tamar sat where the prostitutes would hang out, and she waited. Judah was by himself. He thought no one needed to know what happened on this trip. Judah went and propositioned her, and they haggled over the price. Judah wasn't planning on this pit stop, so he promised to bring payment later. Tamar knew Judah wouldn't keep his promises; plus, she was not after financial compensation. As a guarantee of payment, he gave her his personal identification seal, with its cord and his staff. It's doubtful this was Judah's first time hiring a prostitute. Tamar knew exactly what he would do.

Judah had sex with Tamar without knowing who she was. Just as he had promised, Judah sent his payment, but his Canaanite friend couldn't find the woman. Tamar had snuck away and returned to life as usual. Three months later, Judah found out that she was pregnant and had obviously been unfaithful to her "promised" husband. Judah was so angry with her betrayal that he commanded Tamar to be burned to death. Just as she was about to be dragged out of her home, she took Judah's seal with its cord and staff to identify the father. She was saying, "If you punish me, you have to punish him too." Judah surprised everyone with his response here by saying, "They are mine. She is actually a better person than I am because I didn't give her a husband."

No excuses. After admitting his wrong, he never had sex with her again, but he did treat her sons as his own. From this one-night stand, Tamar had twins: Perez and Zerah. While we're not told the rest of the story yet, God chooses to redeem this incestuous relationship by choosing Perez to become the one who inherits the promised blessing. It's through the line of Perez, King David and ultimately Jesus would come. How phenomenal is that? This whole episode resulted from one bad choice after another, but God still chose to work in spite of their choices and bless them.

REFLECTION QUESTIONS:

The Lord warned His people in Numbers 23:32, "Be sure your sin will find you out." The world Judah lived in didn't have a problem with his actions, but Judah worshipped a different god. Judah should have had a problem with it. He thought he could sneak quietly back to his "other" life, but the consequences followed him. The sins we think no one knows about always break our relationship with God and others. What is a secret sin that no one knows about in your life? How is it actually hurting your relationship with God and others?

_____

_____

_____

_____

_____

What are some things that our culture finds acceptable (or even encourages) that are against the character of the Life-Giver?

_____

_____

_____

_____

While God's redemption of broken situations doesn't excuse the sin, it does demonstrate His unmerited goodness to us. How

have you seen God take a broken situation and make something
beautiful out of it?

_____

_____

_____

_____

_____

GENESIS 39

The story of Joseph is completely amazing. What makes him so amazing? First, God is mentioned more in this chapter than in the previous eight chapters combined! (Most of those chapters are about his dad's life.) Four times in this chapter alone, the Bible says that the Lord was *with* Joseph—that's more times than any other biblical character so far. Joseph's life wasn't the perfect American dream. He was separated from his family, sold into a life of slavery, and unjustly thrown into prison. When Joseph came to Egypt around the age of seventeen, he had to learn a new language, adapt to a new culture, and learn how the Egyptians operated. Joseph found himself working in the home of Potiphar, who was the head of security for Pharaoh. Joseph proved that he was trustworthy, honest, and dependable—totally unlike his deceptive father.

Potiphar saw that Joseph's God was with him and blessed

him. For Potiphar to know of Joseph's God, it meant that Joseph must have been a good reflection of God. This representation was what God had intended when he chose this family. He desired for them to be His witnesses so the rest of the world would see God and be blessed through this family. Joseph was promoted to working "in the house," a place where only the most trusted servants worked.[64] Then he was promoted to manager over Potiphar's house and all his property. Joseph managed the finances, the other slaves, servants, and the farms and kept things running smoothly. Potiphar trusted him so completely that Potiphar didn't even pay attention to his bank account. He just told Joseph when he needed something, and Joseph ran the business. Everything that Joseph managed for Potiphar prospered. Notice that God's prospering of Joseph didn't line his own pockets with cash. Joseph was still a slave. God was using Joseph to bless and prosper those he served. Even if we are in a terrible place in life, God can make us successful and a blessing wherever we are. God measures success and prosperity a bit differently than we often do.

Interestingly, the Bible only mentions three men who were beautiful or handsome. Joseph was the first. Potiphar's wife started to become infatuated with Joseph and decided she wanted to have sex with him. Although Joseph refused, she continued to pester him day after day to sleep with her. His answer is so good. Joseph says, "My boss trusts me and is good to me, so I can't sin against the character of my God!" What a contrast to his brothers back home! Although free, they are enslaved to their lusts and themselves.

Joseph was a slave but ruled over his passions and himself. Joseph was living in a country where sexual integrity was unusual. In a culture that glorified sex, immodesty, and immorality, he was most likely the only one who worshipped a God who desired sexual purity. Joseph called the invitation for what it was (sin) and didn't make excuses to compromise his purity. Most importantly, Joseph knew that all sin was against God and His character, not just his boss. Unlike his father, who primarily feared the consequences of getting caught, Joseph had a real relationship with God and genuinely wanted to do what was right. He chose to accept God's definition of right and wrong. No matter how bad life got or what others believed, he wouldn't eat the fruit.

Joseph made some good moves to protect his purity. He didn't flirt with her to see how far they could go. He didn't hint or put off his answer; he emphatically said no. He put up boundaries to protect himself from temptation. The Bible tells us that Joseph wouldn't even be alone with her without other men in the house with him. One day, however, Potiphar's wife set a trap while the other servants were away. Just as he was heading inside for work, she literally pounced on him, demanding he sleep with her. Joseph didn't deliberate and reason with her; he ran outside as if the house were on fire, leaving his outer garment in her hands. Too often, we hesitate and contemplate giving in or trying to figure out where the "sin" line is, but Joseph had already made up his mind. He wouldn't even consider it. We try to hide our sins by using passwords, going by fake names, hiding in secluded spaces, etc. Joseph made sure he had accountability and that he stayed out in the open. If we want sexual purity, we have to set up boundaries, have accountability, and have someone who has access to all our hiding places.

Potiphar's wife had been rejected again and again. Her obsession turned to anger. She acted quickly to frame Joseph for attempted rape by crying for help and parading Joseph's clothes as proof. She knew that he had a good chance of being executed for her slander, but this was her revenge for being rejected. Human revenge is always more severe than the initial hurt. By the time her husband arrived home, her story had been well rehearsed. She even blamed her husband for allowing this to happen. The word of a slave was of no value.[65] With Potiphar as the captain of the guard, he certainly had the power and right to have Joseph executed for such a charge, so it was unusual for Potiphar to spare his life. Perhaps Potiphar wasn't convinced of Joseph's guilt.

Suddenly, Joseph was in the king's prison. We'd be tempted to cry out, "Where are you, God? Have you abandoned me? I tried to reflect your character and live above reproach! And look where that got me!" However, Joseph continued to trust God even when things didn't make sense and didn't seem fair. Once again, the Lord's presence and favor were with Joseph, and everything he did prospered. The prison manager put Joseph in charge of the other prisoners and just let him do it all! Twice, the text emphasized that God was with Joseph in Potiphar's home; and twice, it re-emphasized that God was with Joseph in prison. Everywhere Joseph went, he prospered because the Life-Giver was always with him.

REFLECTION QUESTIONS:

Joseph allowed God to use him to bless others even when he didn't have those material blessings. We often have the idea that we are willing to give to others until we are even, but Joseph was willing to give so the other had more. Are you willing to give to others when they have more than you?

_____

_____

_____

_____

_____

Joseph took extra precautions to guard his sexual purity. Whether you're married or single, what things can you do to help protect your own sexual purity? (If you're looking for a screen accountability app, consider Covenant Eyes. Find out more at www.covenanteyes.com.)

_____

_____

_____

_____

Joseph was falsely accused of misconduct. Have you ever been falsely accused of something you didn't do? How did you respond? How might Joseph have responded if he had been in your situation?

_____

_____

_____

_____

GENESIS 40

Joseph continued to faithfully stay and serve in the king's prison. Pharaoh, who was the king of Egypt, was offended by his chef and cupbearer, so he had them thrown into prison. What is a cupbearer anyway? As the most important person in the country, Pharaoh was bound to have enemies. It was a real possibility that someone could poison his food, especially the wine. The strong flavor of the wine could mask the taste of the poison, so the cupbearer's job was to guard the wine and taste-test.[66] If the cup had been poisoned, the cupbearer died, not the king. We don't know why the chef and the cupbearer were in prison. While it could have been as simple as burnt bread or a wrong look, it was probably on suspicion of food poisoning or something like that. The captain of the guard put Joseph in charge of these two guys. The captain of the guard—haven't we heard that title before? Remember Potiphar? What was his title? He too was called the captain of the guard. It might likely have been Potiphar himself who entrusted these men to Joseph, leading us to speculate that maybe he was getting less convinced of Joseph's guilt.

Joseph was the boss of these two food attendants. Joseph went to work one morning and noticed something was wrong. He asked them to tell him what their problem was. People consumed with anger and bitterness become so self-absorbed that they don't care about other people's problems, but Joseph cared. They each told him about a dream they had the previous night that was bothering them. While we write off strange dreams as too much pizza or caffeine before bed today, the ancient Middle Eastern cultures believed that the gods communicated to people through dreams.[67] The problem was trying to figure out what the dreams meant. This mystery required a dream expert. The Egyptians and Babylonians had books filled with methodologies and typologies for how dreams were to be interpreted. This is why the two men were upset. They were sitting in prison, not knowing what their future held; and the "gods" sent them a message, but they didn't have access to a translator! Joseph said, "Don't interpretations belong to God?" Joseph was saying, "I know God. He is powerful, and He can tell me the meaning of your dream." Joseph's brothers had teased him and called him the dreamer, and now, he was interpreting other people's dreams. The dream that God sent to each of these men was in their own "cultural" language. He spoke to the cupbearer with fruits, juices, and cups; and He spoke to the baker with bread, baskets, and baked goods.

How do we know that Joseph didn't just make up his interpretations? In this case, time would tell; everyone would know in three days if Joseph (and his God) was right or wrong. Usually, when someone pretends to tell supernatural things, they don't give specific details that can prove them wrong; but after three days, everything happened just like Joseph said it would.

Joseph had asked the cupbearer to tell Pharaoh about him so

he could get out of prison and go home to Canaan. Joseph probably thought, *Surely, this is God's divine way of getting me out of here!* When the cupbearer got out, he got busy with his responsibilities and duties and forgot about Joseph; so there, Joseph waited for another two years. Although the cupbearer might have forgotten about Joseph, God didn't. God wasn't ready for Joseph to be released just yet.

There is something important here in Joseph's interpretations that is often overlooked. Joseph told the truth to both the cupbearer and the baker. It is easy to tell people nice messages about God loving them. It is hard to confront people and tell them a truth that doesn't feel nice. It is amazing how often we hide under the words "blessed are the peacemakers" and don't tell people what they need to hear. There is a difference between being a peacemaker and a peacekeeper. Most people are peacekeepers; they go with the flow, being careful not to rock the boat. This "peacekeeping" sets the stage for all kinds of heartaches and abuses. So many abusers have gotten away with their actions because the people who should have defended the victims were just being peacekeepers. Not many people are peacemakers.

To be a peacemaker, we must be honest even when it hurts. We must be willing to confront and get dirty in people's issues. It's much like a surgeon. We can try to numb the pain of the infection with pain relievers, or we can make the incision and cut out the tumor. It's far easier and less painful in the short term to numb the pain. It's much harder and far more painful in the short term to perform the surgery, but in time, the surgeon helps to restore health and wholeness to the body. It is much easier to be a peacekeeper who only speaks up when it will benefit our agendas. Jesus was definitely not a peacekeeper; he stirred people up wherever He went because He wasn't going to let evil rule. He loved people too much to let them remain broken. He wanted to bring genuine peace to their lives. God doesn't call us to be peacekeepers; He calls us to be peacemakers. Like

Joseph, that often means telling the truth, even when the truth is uncomfortable.

REFLECTION QUESTIONS:

While we don't put much stock in dreams these days and find it kind of funny that they had dream "experts," we do listen to the experts of our day, such as scientists, doctors, and researchers. Joseph's declaration "Do not interpretations belong to God?" still applies to us today. What if we took the attitude, "Does not science, health, or knowledge belong to God?" If we sought Him and put more value in His wisdom rather than relying completely on the experts, how might our lives look different?

_____

_____

_____

_____

Often, when we think of God's favor or blessing in our lives, we think of health, wealth, and prosperity; but God's favor led Joseph to slavery and prison. What blessing was Joseph experiencing? Think about your current situation in life right now. What does this mean for your current circumstances?

_____

_____

_____

_____

_____

How have you felt the pressure to be a peacekeeper versus a peacemaker? When has God called you out of your comfort zone to be a peacemaker? How did it feel at the time? What was the outcome?

_____

_____

_____

_____

_____

GENESIS 41

wo years later—*two years later!*—Joseph was still in prison because the cupbearer forgot about him, but God didn't. Then Pharaoh had a dream that neither he nor his dream experts could figure out. The cupbearer remembered Joseph and told Pharaoh about him. If the cupbearer had gotten Joseph released two years earlier, Joseph would likely have tried to head home and not be available for such a time as this; but since Joseph remained in prison, they knew exactly where to find him.

God was speaking through their dreams, so should we be taking our dreams more seriously? Hebrews 1:1–2 says that God had spoken to us in different ways in times past, but now he speaks to us through His Son. How does God's Son speak to us? We have the Bible that gives us much more clarity about the character of God than they had back then. Since Pentecost, we also have the Holy Spirit who leads us. This way is a far better and clearer method of communication than trying to figure out our dreams!

Pharaoh knew that this was no ordinary "I shouldn't have eaten that before going to bed" kind of dream. Something in his spirit told him that this was an important dream. Joseph was summoned and was soon hearing Pharaoh's problem. Joseph had a lot of faith in God. Before he even heard the dream, Joseph promised an accurate interpretation and gave God the credit. After Pharaoh told him the dream, Joseph quickly interpreted it. God would give them seven years with plenty of food and seven years without food.

From his administrative experience, Joseph gave Pharaoh some advice, "Pick someone discerning and wise." He knew this crisis needed leadership and planning. Joseph gave some practical ideas on how to plan for the crisis. He told Pharaoh to levy a 20 percent food tax, build food storage centers in each city, and have people in charge of each section to collect and store food to distribute later.

Both Pharaoh and his servants saw that something was really different about Joseph. The Spirit of God was with Joseph. Pharaoh was surrounded by priests and religious men, but he didn't have God's presence. This passage is the first time the Bible says someone had the Spirit of God. The literal phrase is "breath of God." Pharaoh saw that there was a living God who was breathing life into Joseph.

Pharaoh said, "I see you have the breath of God in you, so I choose you. You will be the boss of everything and everyone except me, and I want you to do all that stuff you just said." That morning, Joseph was wearing rags; and suddenly, he was wearing the king's approval. He was in chains; and suddenly, he had a gold chain around his neck. He had spent the last several years living in a dungeon, and suddenly, he was the boss of the king's house. Earlier that morning, he was trapped in prison; but now, Pharaoh said, "Without your consent, no man may lift his hand or foot." You can't make this stuff up!

The years in slavery and prison are now beginning to make sense. God's favor in developing him as an administrator wasn't just for Joseph's character development but for the salvation of the whole nation of Egypt and the surrounding nations too. God allowed him to wait in prison for years so that he would be in the right place at the right time. If we haven't figured it out by now, the dreams also remind us that God sees time differently than we do. We are stuck in it, living one day at a time, but God lives and sees outside of time. He sees the end from the beginning and works all things out for good, preparing His people for the challenges ahead.

Joseph was given a wife whose dad was a priest for one of the many Egyptian gods, and she was even named after one of them![68] Pharaoh saw Joseph as a "spiritual" man and gave him a "spiritual" wife. The Bible is silent on her character and how their marriage worked, leaving our imaginations to fill in the gap. Perhaps she too saw the Spirit of God in his life and chose to follow the Life-Giver. They had two sons, and Joseph gave them Hebrew names. The first name was "Making Forgetful," a statement of thanking God for helping him forget his suffering.[69] The next name was "Fruitfulness" in thanking God for blessing him and making him fruitful.[70] As the biblical story unfolds, both of Joseph's sons will become strong tribes within the twelve-tribe nation. If anyone could have played the victim card, it would be Joseph, but he rejected victim-type thinking and sought to make the best of his situation. He chose to be faithful to God and praise Him for using Joseph's pain.

Just as God had told Joseph and Pharaoh, the famine came; and the people ran out of food, so they started buying it from the king's storehouses. People from many countries traveled to buy their food. Talk about some serious trade profit! God was really blessing Pharaoh through Joseph.

Joseph was seventeen when he arrived in Egypt. By the time he turned thirty, he was sitting in prison. Things didn't look very promising, but God was growing Joseph into the kind of man He could trust with a lot of power. God blessed Joseph, and Joseph responded with faithfulness; then, God entrusted Joseph with more. Joseph was getting hands-on experience with managing. He couldn't see God's plan, but it was a "you have to see it to believe it" kind of thing. Pharaoh gave Joseph a new name that likely means "God speaks, and He lives"[71] because he saw that a living God was communicating and breathing life into Joseph. Abraham's descendants were supposed to show the world their God so God could bless the world through them. They were to be missionaries to the other nations. Here, Joseph was showing Egypt who his God was, and God was multiplying their blessings.

REFLECTION QUESTIONS:

Joseph had to grow up fast from the time he was seventeen. In this chapter, he was thirty years old. What might have happened to Joseph if he just felt sorry for himself as a victim of his circumstances and didn't try to follow God?

_____

_____

_____

_____

_____

God was using Joseph's hard times to prepare him for this. What things is God using in your life right now to develop your character?

_____

_____

_____

_____

_____

Pharaoh saw that God was with Joseph. What were some things that Pharaoh saw in Joseph that told Pharaoh God was with him?

_____

_____

_____

_____

_____

GENESIS 42

The story is about to get real as it comes full circle. When you read this, you can't help but think, *Is Joseph getting revenge on his brothers?* The text doesn't tell us the motives behind his actions but purposefully leaves us to wonder and reflect on our own emotional responses as the story unfolds. Joseph knew who they were and who they could become. He knew the family's dysfunctional patterns and wanted to break the cycle. He grew up seeing and hearing of his dad's conflict with Laban, Esau, and Isaac. For most of Jacob's conflicts, Jacob pretended like nothing was wrong, and he didn't work at resolving the issues. Jacob was content to coexist with conflict in his family relationships, but Joseph was not. Joseph wants to be a peacemaker instead of just a peacekeeper. To restore the relationship, trust must be earned back. He knew that you can't trust someone just because you want to; trust must be earned, and he was going to provide his brother with an opportunity to earn it.

At the beginning of the chapter, Jacob realized that the family had to find food or else. He heard that there was food in Egypt and told his sons to stop sitting around and go get some! Jacob noticed that they were "looking at one another," like they knew something he didn't. Elsewhere in this account and in the biblical story, when phrases like this are used, the group is communicating nonverbally.[72] Jacob has been a deceiver all his life and was probably wondering what secret they were hiding from him. It had been twenty years since the brothers sold Joseph, but they hadn't forgotten about him. Jacob wouldn't let his son Benjamin go down to Egypt with the brothers because Joseph's death was still very real in his mind. Notice Jacob only called Benjamin his son, as if the others weren't his sons. Rather than overcoming his dysfunctional parenting style after Joseph's supposed death, Jacob sank even more deeply into it as he was determined not to let Benjamin out of his sight.

The brothers made the long trek to Egypt. When they arrived to buy grain, they bowed down out of respect for Egypt's national leader. Unknown to them, that was Joseph! Remember Joseph's weird dream where all the brothers in a field harvested grain, and then Joseph's grain stood up, and his brother's grain bowed down to his? Joseph instantly recognized them, and this memory flashed before him. Joseph's brothers were literally bowing down to him and asking for some of his grain! God had seen and planned this moment well before Joseph had ever taken that fateful trip to Shechem to find his brothers.

Joseph looked much different as a grown man in Egyptian clothes with an Egyptian accent, so the brothers didn't even have a clue as to his identity. When visitors from the surrounding nations started showing up to buy food, perhaps Joseph had wondered if his own family would be coming at some point. Joseph spoke through an interpreter to hide his identity, and he wasn't very sweet in his manner toward them. Joseph accused them of being spies to see how they would react. His tactics got them talking, and they revealed to Joseph that his father was alive and Brother Benjamin had taken the spot as Dad's favorite. The brothers repeatedly declared that they were honest men, and then they lied to him about what happened to Joseph. Notice how many times in this story the brothers told Joseph and their father that they were honest men. When people repeatedly tell you they are honest, you should be concerned. Joseph put them in prison for three days. Joseph assured them that he believed in God, implying that if they were afraid, they needed to seek God. This revelation should have been a huge relief to them. When Abraham came to Egypt, he was afraid because he knew the Egyptians didn't fear his God and didn't follow God's definition of good and evil. Joseph was telling them that he belonged to God and wouldn't do anything that went against what God said was right, but this didn't comfort them because they didn't belong to God. Joseph knew they wouldn't run to God without fear or pain, so he applied some fear.

After three days, Joseph let them all go except for one. The brothers made the connection that they were suffering because of what they did to Joseph, but that didn't mean they had repented or changed. We can be sorry for the consequences of sin while we are suffering, but as soon as the consequences are gone, we stop being sorry. This type of sorrow is pure selfishness. It doesn't change who we are but will only further destroy us. There is a different kind of sorry, a godly sorrow, where we hate the hell in our hearts and the pain we have inflicted on God and others. The second kind is the only kind that leads us toward full restitution, restoration, and transformation with God and others.[73]

Joseph's brothers' reaction showed that they weren't concerned with what they had done to God, their father, or Joseph; but they were upset that "this distress has come upon" them and that "his blood is now required" of them.[74] They realized they were paying the consequences of their sin, and that was what they didn't like.

As a mental health counselor, I (Ruth) had a life-changing experience when I was in school when my instructor was observing my counseling. She told me that I was stealing from my client! I was shocked! My professor publicly tore apart everything I was doing in that counseling session. She told me that I was trying to steal my client's pain and that his pain was the only thing that would motivate him to change. I thought she was wrong because I was only trying to make him feel better. After beginning my own counseling career, I realized my teacher was absolutely right. Often, we see people broken over the agonizing circumstances in their lives. Most of the time, their tears are not tears of repentance that led them to this moment of pain but tears over the consequences. Once the consequences go away, they are no longer sorry enough to change. While Joseph might have been crying over the fact that his brothers were feeling some remorse, it's more likely that Joseph went away and cried when he heard their conversation because he realized that his brothers were still the broken, selfish beings they were before.

Joseph chose Simeon, the second oldest brother, to be the one to remain in prison until Benjamin could be brought to Egypt. If he was going by tradition and holding the eldest responsible, it should have been Reuben. Maybe he passed over Reuben when Joseph heard that Reuben had actually tried to prevent his brothers from selling him all those years ago. Joseph gave them food and warned them that if they didn't bring their brother back when they came, they would die. Joseph knew they would be back because this was only the first of the seven years of famine. They were hoping the famine was almost over, but Joseph knew it was not. Joseph's actions seem like a mean trick, but Joseph was testing their character to see if they had changed over the past twenty years. So far, it didn't seem as though they were truly sorry beyond the consequences.

Unknown to them, Joseph had their money put back inside their grain sacks. Then he gave them what they needed for their trip home, and they left. These don't seem to be the acts of a revengeful brother but one who cares deeply about them. Putting the money back in the sacks would also be a test to see what they would do with it. When they saw it, they were afraid, probably believing they would be charged with stealing when they returned to Egypt. They told their father, Jacob, everything that happened; and Jacob was miserable. He had a pity party, played the victim card again, and claimed the world was against him. However, think about Joseph's life compared to Jacob's. Jacob hadn't been betrayed by his family, sold as a slave, or thrown in prison. Jacob had a pretty good life in comparison. The pain that Jacob had experienced was mostly due to him living by his own definition of good and evil. Jacob's sons had sold Joseph in response to their father's bad choices and favoritism. Remember, back in the Garden of Eden, humans seized the right to determine good and evil for themselves. Jacob had decided it was "good" to deceive others to get what he wanted. His sons learned from him, and they were deceiving him to get what they wanted. Jacob was just reaping the consequences of his own bad choices and pathetic parenting.

Jacob had been living in a fearful and bitter shell for decades, but he should have been living in faith and hope. Reuben wanted to return to get Simeon and, as a guarantee, offered to let his dad kill his two sons if Benjamin didn't come back safely. Let me just say you know you have dysfunction in your family if you think it would please Grandpa to kill his grandsons in revenge for his own son's death. Jacob wasn't going for it. He talked as if Benjamin were his only son and refused to let him out of his sight, but he was willing to forget about Simeon. Jacob was convinced he would die if Benjamin died, and that is how we end this lovely chapter.

REFLECTION QUESTIONS:

Think of a time when you were hurting because of the consequences of your actions. Did that pain help you make better choices? If so, what would have happened in your relationship with God and others if you hadn't experienced that pain? If it didn't help you change for the better, why not?

_____

_____

_____

_____

_____

Trust isn't something we can give; it must be earned. We can give people more chances, but we can never restore our faith in them without seeing change. They are the only ones who can prove themselves. Have you ever tried to give someone the gift of trust after they broke your trust in them? Could you really do it? How can we help others earn back our faith in them and restore their relationship with us after they have broken our trust?

_____

_____

_____

_____

_____

GENESIS 43

The last chapter ended with Jacob talking to his sons, and this chapter transitions to Israel talking to his sons. This account is the second time we see Jacob take the name that God had told him to take. The prospect of losing his favorite son seems to have pushed Jacob back toward a place of dependence and trust in God.

Jacob and his sons were sitting in Canaan, running out of food. Jacob was probably hoping they could wait out the famine, but it was not happening. So he told them to hit the road. Judah, the fourth born, reminded his dad they weren't going without little Benji because they feared the tyrannical Egyptian ruler. Jacob became upset and blamed them for the current predicament. Why had they been so honest even to tell the Egyptian about Benjamin in the first place? The brothers responded by defending their innocent actions. Judah told him, "We are all going to die if we don't go, and we'll all die if we go without Benjamin. We could have been there and back again if you had just let us go already. Blame me if we don't come back with him." Blaming Judah was more significant than it appeared because Judah was next in line to inherit the promise and blessing after the first three blew it. This action is also the first good thing we have seen Judah do. He was taking some responsibility.

Notice that Jacob, going by Israel again, surrendered and said okay. He gave them the best gifts and lots of money to get what they needed and to come home safely. Jacob had used this tactic before and hoped it would work again. Jacob spoke his final words to them, "May God Almighty give you mercy before the man." Jacob obviously saw this man as godless for doing this to him and his sons, but ironically, the man was God's man, and God was blessing Jacob's family through the man.

When Joseph saw them, he sent his household manager to prepare a really nice dinner for his brothers. They obviously hadn't told Joseph about the money they found in their bags yet, so by the time they arrived at his home, they started panicking. They were convinced this deranged Egyptian ruler was going to conduct an investigation, throw them in prison, and sell them into slavery. When they arrived at Joseph's house, they quickly told the household manager how the money they paid on their first visit mysteriously showed up in their bags. They quickly explained their plan to return it. Joseph must have instructed the manager ahead of time because he responded, "Don't be afraid. Your God and the God of your father gave you that money. We had your payment." Wow! This statement is actually a *huge* thing that an Egyptian would acknowledge and praise the God of Abraham. The Egyptians took every opportunity to prove their gods were superior, but here, he was telling them that their God was powerful. Perhaps Joseph's influence had been rubbing off on him. Then he brought Simeon back to them just as Joseph had promised.

You can just imagine the looks they gave one another after all that happened. Then Joseph's manager gave them water, and they cleaned up for dinner. This greeting wasn't what they were expecting after their last visit. When Joseph came home, they gave him the gifts they had brought and bowed to him once again. Joseph became emotional when he saw his little brother Benjamin and wanted to see his dad too. Then he went off and had a good cry.

Egyptians felt that everyone else was beneath them, so they ate separately from the other people groups. (The ironic thing is that later, the Jewish people would develop a similar pattern where they would not eat with non-Jewish people. Paul addresses this problem in the New Testament.) Since his brothers didn't know that Joseph wasn't an Egyptian, he ate separately from his brothers. However, he had them eat in front of him so that he could watch them. He had the servants seat the brothers at the table in their birth order, with Benjamin in the favorite seat. The brothers were mind-blown and a bit frightened that he would be able to figure this out. If he could "divine" this, what else did he know about them? Then, Joseph had the servants give Benjamin five times the amount of food they had given the brothers. Joseph wanted to see how they would react to Benjamin being the favorite and if they were still the jealous type. When we fail in a certain area of our lives, God will keep testing us in that same area before he trusts us with bigger things. He doesn't give up on us but continues to develop our character as long as we are willing. The chapter ends with the brothers in high spirits from the banquet.

REFLECTION QUESTIONS:

Jacob and his sons had so much anxiety over the entire situation, even though God had already promised Jacob that he and his sons would be protected and prosper. Although they were facing difficult days, God was in complete control. How would their lives have been different if they had just trusted God's promises even when they couldn't see what He was doing?

_____

_____

_____

_____

_____

What promises has God made to us that we aren't fully living in? Would we have less anxiety if we trusted Him completely?

_____

_____

_____

_____

_____

GENESIS 44

After a good night's rest, the brothers were ready to return home. As the donkeys were being loaded, Joseph made a plan to test his brothers' character again. Joseph had his manager put Joseph's silver cup in Benjamin's sack and their money back in each of the brothers' sacks. Not long after they had left, Joseph had the manager go after them and say, "Why do you think it is good to do evil to someone who has been good to you? You took a very special cup that belongs to my master." It was the practice at that time to use special cups to learn supernatural things based on how the sediments fell in the cup. We don't know if Joseph actually did this, but the point is that the brothers understood this was a *very* special cup. With confidence, the brothers said, "We wouldn't do that. We brought back the money we had last time. We wouldn't steal any valuables. Come and search us. If any one of us has it, you can kill him, and the rest of us will be your slaves." The manager said, "Okay, but only the man who has it will be the slave, and the rest of you can go."

It is good to see that the brothers trusted one another. After all, they had been through a lot with this unhinged Egyptian; no one would be ignorant enough to steal from him! Instead of looking around and wondering who had the cup, they didn't hesitate because they knew they were innocent. The brothers quickly opened their bags, and lo and behold, the cup was in Benjamin's sack! The brothers' hearts sank. How did the cup get there? Was Benjamin really so foolish as to steal it? Or had God miraculously restored their silver but was now punishing them for their past sins?

Benjamin was going to have the same fate Joseph had. Would the brothers use the opportunity to rid themselves of the new favorite child? Would they seek an escape to save their own lives? Or were they repentant for what they had done? Would they seek a way to save little Benjamin? The brothers tore their clothes (a cultural sign of anguish and sorrow). The manager had told the brothers they were free to go home, but *all* the brothers loaded up their donkeys and went back. They went back to Joseph's house and fell on the ground. Joseph said, "What did you do? Do you think I'm a fool?" The brothers had been framed, but they didn't return with excuses or demanding justice; they returned, publicly confessing that they were the ones deserving of punishment (not for the cup but for what they had done to their other brother decades ago). The brothers had sold Joseph because he hurt their pride, so they made him a slave. Now, they gave up their pride to keep their other brother from being a slave.

Judah seems to be a different person than he was earlier. He said, "I have no excuses. This situation is beyond our ability to make right. How can we make it right? God knows our sins and has exposed them. This crisis has happened because of our evil behavior, so all of us will be your servants, not just the one with the cup." Judah recognized that this crisis was happening to them because of what they had done to Joseph, and they were all to blame for that. Time does not erase sin.

This commitment is significant because these men were now wealthy with statuses and families of their own, but now, they were agreeing to be slaves. While confession of wrongdoing is the first step, it still doesn't demonstrate if their hearts have changed toward their father or the favorite child. Joseph said, "No, just Benjamin. The rest can go back in peace to your father." That whole "peace with your father" bit was not a random comment. Joseph had surely been wondering how they had explained his absence to their father when Joseph had not gone home twenty-two years ago.

Judah tried again with the longest-recorded speech in the book. He started with a little flattery and then pleaded his case again with more fervor and conviction. What do you think Joseph thought when Judah recounted Jacob's words, "Surely, my son is torn to pieces"? Notice that Judah didn't lie; he just repeated what Jacob said and then added that he, Judah, hadn't seen Joseph since. We see no bitterness that Benjamin was the favorite or that Rachel was the only wife mentioned. Notice what Judah identifies as his motivation. He said he was worried that Jacob, his father, would be so broken if they came back without Benjamin that Jacob would probably die. They cared too much to allow him to experience this suffering again. This attitude is a huge change!

When they sold Joseph, they were bitter because of their father's favor toward Joseph, and they didn't care how much it hurt their father. Judah, on behalf of all the brothers, acknowledged that Benjamin was the favorite, but they still didn't want to hurt him. Then Judah asked to be substituted as a slave in place of Benjamin. Who was it that suggested they sell Joseph into slavery twenty-two years ago? And who was it that was now offering to be a slave for his brother? Judah. Twenty-two years ago, Judah wanted Joseph's place in their father's eyes, so he suggested slavery. At this point, Judah wanted Benjamin's place in slavery to protect their father. Truly, this crisis with Benjamin had finally brought the brothers to a point of confession, repentance, and humility. The test had been answered. The ball was now in Joseph's court.

REFLECTION QUESTIONS:

Have you ever been falsely accused? It is interesting that Joseph had been falsely accused, and now he is accusing his brothers. Did his brothers respond the same way he did? How did you respond?

_____

_____

_____

_____

We are all tempted to think that if we just forget about our sin, time will make it go away, but it never goes away or becomes less. It is always just as big in God's eyes and in the eyes of those we hurt. What sin in your life have you been trying to hide with time? Today, meet with a spiritual mentor and confess it to them. Ask them to pray with you as you confess to God and seek to make it right. Ask your mentor what they believe is the best way to make it right. This process is called restitution. We can't earn forgiveness, but we need to do everything in our power to restore what we have broken.

_____

_____

_____

_____

_____

GENESIS 45

Now the story gets good. With Judah's expression of self-sacrifice for Benjamin and their father, Joseph couldn't hold out on them any longer. He made all his Egyptian servants leave, but he cried so loud that they all heard him anyway. The news of the arrival of Joseph's family reached Pharaoh. The secret was out.

Imagine the scene from the brothers' perspectives. You have returned to the malicious Egyptian who spoke roughly to you for no apparent reason; then he thinks you're a spy, throws you in prison, and keeps one of your brothers as a hostage. Then, on the next visit, he throws a party for you and treats you like guests of honor. Now you're back trying to negotiate slavery; and the next thing you know, he starts crying. You probably think this guy has issues! Then, through his tears, he says something about being Joseph and his dad being alive.

Once the reality of that statement sank in, the brothers were so mind-blown and terrified that they didn't say anything. So Joseph continued, "Come here! Yes, I am Joseph. You sold me to Egypt [a fact that only Joseph and his brothers knew], but don't beat yourselves up about it. God actually sent me here to be a life sustainer. We have had a famine for two years, and it will continue for another five years. God sent me here for *you*—to preserve the life of our family. I am now the guardian of Pharaoh and the one who rules Egypt."

So was Joseph in Egypt because his brothers did evil or because God brought him there? The answer is *yes*, both! Joseph's approach was "You did evil, but God ..." When someone hurts us, we are either tempted to get angry about it or pretend it didn't happen. The right thing to do is to acknowledge the evil for what it is and then say, "But God." We need to acknowledge that He turns everything for the good of His people who love and follow Him.[75] This gives us no excuse for lasting anger, resentment, or victimhood but sets us free! After the pain, we will never be the same as we were before; but through God, we can always come through it better than we ever were without it.

When Joseph said, "God meant it to preserve our family and save our lives by a great deliverance," Joseph was talking about the famine, but God also brought Israel here to grow a nation. This thought is mind-blowing. If the family had stayed in Canaan, they probably would have married the Canaanites and soon become one of them, but God kept them in a land where the other people wouldn't marry them. Few Egyptians would intermarry or mix with the Hebrew people, thus preserving the Israelite distinction from the other nations. This separation helped preserve their history and belief in God. This family would end up living in the land of Egypt for four hundred years, turning into a great nation, but that's the story of the next book.

Joseph didn't need any revenge on his brothers. He left that up to God, and God got the "best revenge." Human revenge leaves us more broken and with more suffering than before. It never satisfies, and it is never enough. If we are willing, God desires to take our brokenness and the evil inflicted on us and turn it into a blessing that we could never have received or appreciated without the trial. Then, we, in turn, give that treasure to others, and everyone is blessed. Nothing in this world is more enjoyable than giving life and healing to others. This life and healing come from the wholeness we receive when God heals us and brings us back to life.

I (Ruth) once talked to a woman who had been a victim of child sex trafficking. She said the best part of her life was pouring herself into helping other victims find wholeness and healing. She said she wouldn't give up the pain she went through because now God was using it to be the most rewarding part of her life. That is the best revenge, and it is God's revenge because He is the Life-Giver.

Joseph then told his brothers to get their father and their families and hurry back to Egypt. He told them not to even worry about all their possessions, for they would be given the best! He told them that if their father didn't believe them, they should have Benjamin tell him. He cried and hugged all of them, and they talked because they had lots of catching up to do. Pharaoh heard of it and was happy for Joseph. He sent lots of carts and wagons to bring Joseph's family and their belongings to Egypt. The king promised them the best of the best: a place where the grass still grew amid the famine. Joseph gave them lots of stuff and told them not to overthink things or dwell on the guilt of the past. To go back to the famine-stricken desert of Canaan with all the delicacies of a five-star restaurant would have felt unreal!

When the brothers had left Canaan, their father was Israel. When they returned to Canaan, they found he was Jacob again. Perhaps he began to doubt and despair, believing he would never see Benjamin again. However, after they told him about Joseph, his "spirit revived."[76] With this newfound hope, Jacob once again returned to the name of Israel.

REFLECTION QUESTIONS:

This was the perfect opportunity for Joseph to get revenge by enslaving his brothers, but he chose God's revenge and blessed them once they proved themselves. Is there anyone in your life with whom you want revenge? Pray right now and surrender that to God. What does God want you to do about it?

_____

_____

_____

_____

Think of all the torment Jacob or Israel went through worrying about himself and his children. It is a little mind-blowing because God had worked everything out to the smallest detail. What might Jacob's life have looked like if he had brought his anxiety to God and had trusted Him?

_____

_____

_____

_____

We are all part of the Bible story. The Bible is our story too. Someday we will see how God was working all our situations out like he was working out Jacob's. How can we live differently than Jacob did so we have trust, peace, and joy?

_____

_____

_____

_____

_____

GENESIS 46

This chapter begins when Jacob started off toward Egypt with his family and everything they had. Notice that Jacob was still going by the name Israel at this point. A day or two into their journey, Israel stopped for the night at Beersheba. This spot was on the southern edge of Canaan. Here, there was only desert between them and Egypt. While we're not told what Israel was thinking, perhaps he was wondering if leaving the Promised Land was really the right course of action. Would God really lead them away from this place? Israel was already 130. If they left, would he ever return home?

Earlier in chapter 21, a Philistine king with the title Abimelech went to Abraham and said, "I am afraid of you because God is with you. Promise me peace, and you can have this well," and they swore an oath. Again, in chapter 26, another Philistine king with the same title Abimelech had gone to Isaac and said, "I am afraid of you because God is with you. Promise me peace, and you can have this well," and they swore an oath. Both of these incidents happened here at Beersheba. Now Israel was at Beersheba, perhaps wondering if God would be with them in a foreign land. Israel offered sacrifices to God and went to bed. That night, God told him in a dream, "Don't be afraid because the God your dad served is with you. I will give you peace, and your children will be like an overflowing well and develop into a nation in Egypt. I will take you down to Egypt. I will be with you there, and I will bring you out again. Joseph shall put his hand on your eyes." More than forty years before, God met Jacob in a dream and assured him that he was to leave Canaan to find a wife. Now, God met him again and assured him he was to go to the land of Egypt.

God would use Egypt to keep the family of Israel separate from other peoples as they developed into a nation. He didn't want this family to intermarry with other nations because He wanted them to keep their faith. Earlier at Joseph's banquet and again at the end of this chapter, we see that the Egyptians didn't want to mingle much with them because the sons of Israel were shepherds. The Egyptians were one of the more exclusive people groups during this time.[77] God was putting Israel in the perfect place to grow without mixing much with the locals.

Why did God say to Israel that Joseph would put his hand on Israel's eyes? This phrase was a cultural way of saying that Joseph would take care of his father and would be there at Israel's death. Israel's faith was at its best when he decided they were all going to Egypt. Should there be questions later, Israel and his family know they have gone down according to God's will. When things became difficult in the coming years, his descendants would need that assurance. Israel didn't leave anyone behind or split his resources on this journey. Unlike the Jacob with whom we have become familiar who had been afraid to put all his eggs in one basket, Israel went forward in confidence.

The text records the descendants of Israel who went down to Egypt: sixty-six in all, not including their wives or servants. As names are mentioned later in the biblical story, it will help the reader connect them to families. The sons of Judah will be of particular interest and importance because this will be the line from which Jesus descends.

Notice how slowly things seem to develop. God told Abraham he would be the father to a great nation. At least 25 years later, Abraham had his first descendant for this nation. Sixty years later, Isaac has Jacob. Around 60 years later, Jacob begins having his twelve sons and a daughter. It's been around 215 years since God first gave the promise to Abraham, and we're only up to seventy descendants (plus wives). Things hadn't progressed very quickly, but the population was about to explode. God has been more concerned with developing the character of the patriarchs and making sure they are in the right place before establishing them as a nation.

As the family approached, Israel asked Judah to be the one who led the way when they arrived. Remember, he was the fourth born, but he had been taking the lead in the family for a while now. He blew it pretty good earlier, but he seemed to be taking more responsibility for his actions and his family. Joseph could not wait for his father to arrive and rushed out in his chariot to meet his father. After twenty-two years, Jacob and Joseph had an emotional reunion. Joseph had a plan for the family to live separately in Goshen and raise their animals away from the Egyptians. All that was needed was Pharaoh's permission.

This chapter began with Jacob going by Israel. However, when God talked to him, God called him Jacob, and he responded to Jacob. From that point on, he would go by Jacob until he got to Egypt and saw Joseph. Then, once again, Jacob went back to Israel for a time.

REFLECTION QUESTIONS:

Jacob was nervous about leaving his home and traveling to Egypt. He likely knew he would die in this foreign land. How has God called you out of your comfort zone to follow Him? How has God sustained and strengthened you in these times?

_____

_____

_____

_____

Why do you think God keeps repeating these words to Jacob or Israel, "Don't be afraid because the God your dad served is with you. I will give you peace, and your children will be like an overflowing well and develop into a nation"?

_____

_____

_____

_____

We often forget God's promises, especially in times of political unrest or when the unexpected happens. What are some of the situations where you have a tendency to forget God's promises? What are some of God's promises that you tend to forget? How can we learn to live daily in those promises?

_____

GENESIS 47

At the end of the last chapter, Joseph prepared his brothers for how they were to meet and respond to Pharaoh. In this chapter, Joseph took five brothers and his father to meet Pharaoh. The brothers' statements implied that they had no intention to stay long-term or become powerful among the Egyptians. Pharaoh's response was pretty amazing! Joseph's family asked for the land of Goshen, and Pharaoh said, "Whatever land in Egypt you want is yours. Take the best for your family, and if Joseph thinks they know what they're doing, he is welcome to put them in charge of my animals too." This act provided financial support for the family during the famine and gave legitimacy to their setting up camp in Goshen.

Jacob was given an incredible opportunity to pray for Egypt's national leader. What was up with Jacob's response to Pharaoh? Notice he went back to being Jacob; there was no Israel here. This response was one of the most telling moments of Jacob's life. After Pharaoh's incredible gifts, Jacob had a pity party about how hard his life had been and then said to Pharaoh, "Bless you." This response is so pathetic. It is heartbreaking when you realize that Jacob's hardships were a result of his own choices to decide good and evil apart from God. Jacob had been reaping the natural consequences of his own bad choices, and now he felt sorry for himself. Pharaoh didn't respond out loud to Jacob here, but we can't help but see the irony. Pharaoh, who was considered a god of Egypt, had met Joseph and recognized that in Joseph, "God speaks and lives."

Joseph had made it clear that he was no god but had been blessed by God. In Egypt, the blessing of godhood was seen as going from the father to his son. Now, Pharaoh was excited to meet the father of his blessed right-hand man. Pharaoh knew that he, Pharaoh, had been blessed by Joseph's God, so he offered Joseph's father the best of his land and possessions. And what did Jacob say? "My life is miserable." Not once in the conversation did Jacob even mention God. What can Pharaoh assume? He knew Joseph was a man blessed by God, but apparently, that blessing skipped Jacob.

While Jacob's blessing of Pharaoh was unrecorded, it didn't seem to have been much better than their brief conversation. Jacob ended with a lame "bless you" to Pharaoh. More irony here. If it weren't for God's blessing on Jacob, then Joseph wouldn't have had God's wisdom and ability to help Egypt. Egypt would have been suffering and starving like the rest of the region, but because God made a covenant with Abraham and his descendants, the nation of Egypt was prospering. Remember when God told Abraham and his descendants that the reason He was blessing them was so the rest of the world would be blessed through them? Egypt and the rest of that region were now surviving this famine because of God's covenant with Abraham. Now Pharaoh was sharing God's blessing back with Jacob, and Jacob said, "Bless you." Because of God's continued blessing, Jacob's family would live in the best land in Egypt and have plenty of food in the middle of a famine. Jacob seems to be so blinded by his victimhood that he doesn't even understand how this was God's plan playing out. All he saw was his own misery, and Jacob seemed to be crediting his current good luck to a different god, Pharaoh.

After noting that Jacob's family had been settled and provided for, the text focuses on all the blessings that God gave Pharaoh through Joseph. Pharaoh became rich and powerful by selling the stores of grain to the Egyptians and the surrounding nation. After all the money had been used to buy grain, the Egyptians sold their cattle and then their land to Pharaoh. Joseph then leased their land back to them and had them pay a 20 percent tax to Pharaoh. Most of the time, when there is a national crisis, the government tends to increase its power.

After the famine, Jacob and his family continued to live in Goshen for another twelve years (seventeen so far in Egypt), and God blessed them exceedingly in both possessions and children. The gift of children had been slow in this family, but that was changing as God was ready to begin growing them into a nation just as He had promised. Notice it says that Jacob, not Israel, lived in Egypt for seventeen years. His family and possessions were growing. Right before he died, Israel told Joseph not to bury him in Egypt but to take him back to the family crypt. He was so adamant on this point that he made Joseph promise in the same way that his grandfather Abraham made his servant promise to get a wife for Isaac from his kinfolk.

Why was this such a big deal to Jacob? He wanted to go home to the land God promised because he knew Egypt was not the land promised by God. This request was a declaration to all his family that they shouldn't get too comfortable. Egypt was not their home. In his death, he was seeking to point his kids back to God's promises. He seemed to be ending on a good note, acknowledging that he knew he was blessed by God and that he had received the covenant blessing.

REFLECTION QUESTIONS:

When Jacob appeared before Pharaoh, it was the perfect opportunity to tell Pharaoh about his God, but he was too focused on himself. When was the last time you told others what God has been doing in your life? What keeps you from doing this?

_____

_____

_____

_____

_____

God abundantly blessed Pharaoh and Egypt through Joseph. When people follow God's way, there are usually "spill-over blessings" to those they come in contact. How have you experienced unmerited blessing through the other's relationship with Jesus? In what ways is your relationship with Jesus spilling over to those you come in contact with?

_____

_____

_____

_____

_____

Throughout Jacob's life, we have seen him flip back and forth between Jacob (deceiver) and Israel (God wrestler), often reflecting the spiritual highs and lows in his life. Jacob never seems to be able to fully stay surrendered to God. Is there a Jacob and an Israel in you? In the New Testament, Jesus came to set us free from the sinful, deceptive nature that is in all of us. To be completely free from this, you must completely surrender everything in your life: your plans, your reputation, your possessions, etc. You have to be *all in* because God is *all in*. This surrender isn't just a one-time deal. It is a daily thing, but the first time is the hardest. Totally surrendering to God daily is the only way to truly be alive. Have you surrendered everything to God, or are you still holding on like Jacob?

_____

_____

_____

_____

_____

GENESIS 48

srael was dying and sent for Joseph. Jacob had always treated Joseph as his favored firstborn and intended to bless him first. He seemed to think the promised blessing would come through Joseph's line as he blessed Joseph's sons. Israel began by referring to the name that God had used of Himself when God appeared to him for the first time at Bethel. Then Jacob repeated the exact same words that God first said to him. Jacob called Joseph's sons his own, just as Reuben and Simeon were his first and second children. Manasseh and Ephraim would be at the head of the family. Israel then recalled the death of Joseph's mother, Rachel.

Joseph, who had been in a place and position where most people bowed to him, was now bowing to his father. Joseph pushed his sons, who are probably between the ages of twenty-four and thirty, to his near-blind father. Usually, the father would be blessing his son directly; but here, we see that Israel was blessing Joseph by blessing Joseph's sons. Israel didn't bless them according to their birth order. The right hand was a symbol of authority and blessing, so Israel's right hand should have been on Joseph's firstborn, but Jacob was led by God to cross his arms and bless the younger, Ephraim, with the hand of favor. Joseph objected, probably thinking his nearly blind father had made a mistake, but Israel reassured him there was no mistake. The younger would become greater than the older. We've already noted in our journey through Genesis that God seldom picks who we expect or according to cultural custom. This pattern will continue as the biblical story continues to unfold. Later in the biblical story, we see that both sons became important tribes in Israel; but the younger, Ephraim, became the largest and most prominent, just as Israel had blessed them.

This whole scene is kind of a déjà vu moment as the almost-blind father was blessing his sons, but he picked the younger for the bigger blessing. Remember Isaac choosing Jacob over Esau? Then Israel praised God for his provision and protection but didn't say anything about his faithfulness to God. Remember when Jacob told Pharaoh that his life had been short and evil? Now, he was telling his family that God had sustained and directed his life and redeemed the evil.

During the blessing, Israel told Joseph he would get a "double portion." In the centuries that followed, each of Israel's sons became a tribe in the nation of Israel, but Joseph's sons each became a tribe of their own, inheriting more property and more power than the other brothers; but like Abraham, Isaac, and Jacob, they wouldn't see the fulfillment of the blessing and promise in their own lifetime. It would be over four hundred years before they would return to dwell in the Promised Land.

As wonderful as the double portion may be, the best blessing that Israel passed along was the promise that God would be with them. There is nothing better that a parent can give their kids than for their kids to grow up in a home where God lives. When parents surrender to God's version of right and wrong, the presence of the Life-Giver also lives in that home. When the presence of the Life-Giver lives in a home, there are no limits to what kind of evil God can redeem. Jacob had blown it many times and often became focused on the wrong things, resulting in much heartache. However, it's never too late to turn to Him and allow His presence to begin redeeming our family. We need His presence to be fully satisfied. If you want your children to have the best life, teach them how to submit to the Life-Giver. The kind of happiness that He gives rarely comes in the form of lots of possessions, but what He gives is priceless.

Notice that the text never mentions Joseph taking more than one wife or having children with any woman other than Asenath. Joseph was living in a culture and in a position where he could have had lots of women. After all, Joseph's own father had four wives. Living in Egypt, Joseph's two sons grew up in a completely pagan culture. They had been the only Hebrew people and likely the only worshippers of their God until the rest of the family came to town. Recall that Joseph's wife was the daughter of a priest, and her name most likely refers to the Egyptian goddess Neith.[78] She was given to him by Pharaoh when Joseph was promoted from prison to rule. In light of his wife's upbringing and the culture in which they were living, Joseph must have been very involved in the life of his sons because we see that they were very familiar with their Hebrew heritage, and they embraced their father's God. Joseph was a very busy man with a lot of pressure, but he prioritized being a good father, and it paid off. Both Ephraim's and Manasseh's kids became large tribes and went back to the land of Canaan.

REFLECTION QUESTIONS:

Like Joseph, are there aspects of your own family that are dysfunctional? Contrast Jacob's and Joseph's choices. What are some things that Joseph did differently to follow God? How did these choices affect their kids? How did these choices change the course of their families?

_____

_____

_____

_____

_____

Joseph raised a God-honoring family in a pagan society. What negative cultural influences do families face today? How can we be involved in the lives of our families to overcome these influences and train our children in godliness?

_____

_____

_____

_____

GENESIS 49

Wow! This chapter is so packed full of prophecy that only a divine being unbound by time could reveal it so concisely. For our purpose, we are only scratching the surface.

After first blessing Joseph's sons, Israel gathered all his sons together and delivered his last words as a prophecy about what would happen to them and their descendants. Notice he called the sons of Jacob together and told them to listen to their father, Israel. He knew they were the sons of a deceiver. Overall, they were a group of deceptive men, but he wanted them to obey the father who wrestled with God. How many parents want their children to "do as I say, not as I do"? Jacob was acknowledging in this quote that he was both. He was both the deceiver and the one with whom God wrestled. God does not desire for us to live in this state of constant tension between our own desires and what is right. As the biblical story unfolds, this will be a constant problem until God Himself provides the solution to this dilemma.

Jacob went on to prophesy some events. God had done this several times, but this was the first time we saw Him doing it through a man in the Bible story. Israel started with Reuben because he was the firstborn. He called it for what it was and said, "You are not the spiritual leader. You were meant to be, but you decided to determine good and evil for yourself. Therefore, your descendants will not lead your brothers. God isn't giving you the authority of the firstborn." As the story continues, we don't see any prophets, judges, or kings who come from Reuben's line.

Israel continued with the rest of Leah's children. Simeon and Levi were next in the prophecy. Jacob said, "Neither of you are spiritual leaders either. You are angry, cruel men, and your descendants will be scattered among the other tribes." Notice that God was more concerned about their anger, cruelty, and self-will than what they did with it. There was a disease inside of them that infected whatever they touched. Not only did they kill people, but they were also daily inflicting others with pain from the disease growing inside them. God was going to scatter them to prevent them from banding together and inflicting mass pain. This prophecy played out with Simeon's kids while they were wandering the desert in the book of Numbers. They were the third largest tribe when they left Egypt, and thirty-five years later, they were the smallest tribe.[79] They lost over half of their population during that time and ended up having to share their land with Judah because they were so weak.[80] The scattering prophecy for Levi ended up being a blessing. When the Israelites left Egypt, Levi's kids refused to worship the golden calf,[81] so they became scattered around the tribes in forty-eight cities across the nation as the priests or preachers for each group. Somewhere along the way, Levi's kids decided they weren't deciding good and evil for themselves, and God turned their curse into a blessing.

Now we come to Judah. Judah didn't start out very promising, but he did make some positive changes later on, and God chose Judah's kids to become the leaders in the family. There is a ton of prophecy in verses 8–12, and whole books have been written on the fulfillment of these verses. Judah's kids would be the kings and rulers of Israel, but most of this prophecy is actually about Jesus. Yes, Jesus has been all over the book of Genesis!

Jacob then skipped the birth order to the tenth-born Zebulun, but there was a method to his madness. He was focusing on Leah's kids in their birth order. The tribe of Zebulun ended up settling on a piece of land between the Mediterranean Sea and the Sea of Galilee.[82] Issachar's promise wasn't very flattering. His children would end up in a fertile land but a land that was often controlled by other nations, yet they would stay and serve. After giving a prophetic word about Dan, Israel cried out, "I wait for your salvation!" Israel seemed to be grieved over the direction Dan was heading. Later, Dan's kids would introduce idolatry to Israel and eventually become a center for idol worship. Next up were Gad's kids. They became good soldiers and gained a reputation for being fierce in battle during the conquest of the Promised Land.[83] Asher's kids later inherited fertile land that would produce a lot of olive oil, a staple in the ancient Israeli diet and a key ingredient in making bread.[84] While scholars are not sure how the prophecy ended up playing out with Naphtali's kids, the tribe of Naphtali would end up near the Sea of Galilee.[85]

In the previous chapter, Jacob already prophesied about Joseph's descendants; so here, he focused on what God had done through Joseph. Then Jacob went on to list five things about who God is. Lastly, Israel addressed Benjamin. Although Benjamin's kids would be one of the smaller tribes, they earned a reputation for being great warriors. Some leaders who would descend from

Benjamin were Ehud, King Saul, Jeremiah, and the Apostle Paul in the New Testament.[86]

It is amazing that none of these families disappeared or died out during the next four hundred years. They each became significant tribes. This timespan is longer than the United States has been a nation! How many of us have stayed in groups with our families from four hundred years ago?

Jacob could have had a really nice tomb in Egypt, but he knew he didn't belong there. He wanted to be buried in the Promised Land with his ancestors and where his descendants would one day reside. He believed that God would take them back.

Did you notice something familiar about the prophecy Israel said to Dan? Dan would be like a snake that would bite the horse's heel and injure the rider. Remember God's promise to the snake? The snake would bite the man's heel, but the man would crush his head. Israel had this moment when he probably realized the parallel as he was talking to Dan. He stopped the prophecy and cried out to God for a savior to rescue them. Israel realized that his descendants were going to grow hell in their hearts and inflict wounds on others, just like the serpent from the garden. He knew they had no hope unless God sent a deliverer who would save them from the snake. As English readers, we don't catch the Hebrew word for *salvation* is Yeshua, and Yeshua translated back into English is Jesus. When Jacob said, "I wait for your *salvation*, O Lord," he was literally saying "I wait for your *Jesus*" to save us.

Israel knew Dan's descendants would embrace and grow the disease of the snake, and they needed a Jesus to save them from themselves. Whenever Jacob talked about God throughout his life, he called Him "the God of my fathers" or "the God of Abraham and Isaac." Now, for the first time, on his deathbed, Israel called God his own. While talking to Joseph, Jacob referred to "the God of Jacob and the God of your father." Finally, Jacob owned up to his failures and God's faithfulness and begged his sons not to listen to the snake but to follow the Life-Giver.

REFLECTION QUESTIONS:

What five things does Israel's statement to Joseph reveal about God? What might your life look like if you truly believed these things about God?

_____

_____

_____

_____

_____

Israel wants his children to "do as I say, not as I do." Does this usually work in parenting or in any relationship?

_____

_____

_____

_____

_____

If we really want people to live a certain way, we have to really believe it and live it. If we don't really live it, we don't really believe it. Do other people see you living what you say you believe? What needs to change in your life for others to see God in you?

_____

_____

_____

_____

_____

GENESIS 50

This chapter opens with God's words to Jacob being fulfilled: "Joseph will put his hands on your eyes." Joseph seemingly mourned his father's death more than any of the other brothers. The whole nation of Egypt mourned with Joseph for his father for seventy days. This bereavement demonstrates to us that he was considered a very special man, for the people would mourn the death of Pharaoh for seventy-two days![87] Joseph did as his dad wanted and took Israel's body to Canaan. This funeral procession was huge and super dramatic! Look at all the people who made this journey to bury Israel: Israel's family, the servants in Pharaoh's house, and the elders of Egypt with a small army all made this road trip for the funeral. Even the Canaanites saw the elaborate ceremony and were impressed. The sons did exactly as their father wanted by burying him in the same place their grandparents and great-grandparents were buried.

After the mourning was over and the brothers had returned to Egypt, they started to get scared that Joseph would take revenge on them for what they did to him. They were afraid that it was only his love for Dad that kept him nice. So the sons of the deceiver came up with a deceptive story. They sent a messenger boy ahead to Joseph, saying, "Dad told us to tell you that you are supposed to be nice to us and not hurt us. You might not have been there when he said that, but he did." Then Joseph cried. He thought his brothers were finally learning to trust the Life-Giver, but this stunt just proved they were still just trying to protect themselves. Several times already, Joseph had told them not to be afraid and not quarrel over the past.

Joseph had the power to take any kind of revenge he wanted, but he had already given it over to God and had forgiven them. He told his brothers again, "Do not be afraid of me. You are in God's hands, not mine. You meant it for evil against me, but God meant it for good to nurture and sustain life for many people. Don't be afraid. I am His image bearer and will continue to be a life nurturer and sustainer for you and your families." God is the great redeemer. He took the pain and hell the brothers inflicted on Joseph and used it to save their own lives and the lives of their families. God didn't stop there. He multiplied the good to spread life to the nation of Egypt and surrounding peoples. Joseph's testimony exemplifies God's promise to Abraham that He would bless Abraham's family so that the rest of the world would also be blessed through them. This is God's revenge.

When Joseph died, he could have insisted on being buried in a big fancy place. What is the first thing that pops up in your head when someone says Egypt? Fancy tombs. We could be visiting Joseph's pyramid in Egypt today if he wanted a tomb, but Joseph didn't want to go big; he wanted to go home. In the same way his father had requested not to be left in Egypt, Joseph had his bones put in a coffin that would be sent to the Promised Land when his family made their journey back. Little did he know, his bones would wait in Egypt for almost four hundred years as a reminder to the people that this was not their home. Here, the book leaves us with so many questions! Were Joseph's bones taken back to Canaan? When will Israel become a nation? When will God fulfill His promise and give them Canaan? How will all nations be blessed through this family? And perhaps most importantly, how will God reconcile our deceitful hearts to Himself without destroying us in the process? Thankfully, we have the answers as the biblical story continues.

The beginning of Genesis tells us about God creating a world where beauty, life, and giving are what is good. Adam, or humanity, ate the fruit from the tree. Adam determined that he was going to decide what was good and evil. Throughout the book, we read story after story of more Adams embracing evil and calling it good. The evil that Adam embraced is a disease that infected his own life and the lives of everyone with whom he came in contact. The effects were devastating as the people inflict hell on one another through rape, murder, incest, abuse, and every kind of evil. At the end of Genesis, we see Joseph say to his brothers, "You thought it was good to do evil, but God took your evil and turned it into something good." This one phrase sums up the book of Genesis and is a prophetic statement for the rest of the Bible.

In chapter 3, the snake inflicted evil on us, but God didn't give up. If we surrender to God, He takes what the snake meant as evil and turns it into something good. God gets the best revenge in the form of *redemption*. And God's redemption has no limit to the amount of good that comes from it. Once we accept His definition of good and evil, there is no one and no situation that God can't breathe life into because He is the Life-Giver!

REFLECTION QUESTIONS:

How have you seen God take something that was intended to harm you and turn it into something good? If you haven't, what is the hurt you are currently experiencing? Joseph didn't know how God would use his trials, but He surrendered them to God and remained faithful. If we surrender our own trials to Him, God will bring good out of them as well.

_____

_____

_____

_____

_____

Joseph suffered, yet God worked it together both for Joseph's good and for the good of others. How can God use your trials to become a blessing to others?

_____

_____

_____

_____

_____

Pause and reflect on Jacob's life. Think about the many times Jacob did not reflect God's image, yet God continued to chase after and wrestle with him. What does this say about who God is? Jacob is the story of each of us at some point in our lives. God keeps pursuing us even when we fail to reflect His image. What does this say about who God thinks you are?

_____

_____

_____

_____

_____

AFTERWORD

As we close this study into the Life-Giver of Genesis, we trust your walk with the Lord has been strengthened, your understanding of His character deepened, and your perspective on your own identity enriched. We wrote this after realizing that so many people were struggling with a personal identity crisis. This crisis went deeper than themselves and was actually based on their misunderstanding of who God is. No one can truly know who they are until they have a good understanding of the one who created them. Our prayer from the very beginning was that this book would become a conduit for deepening your understanding and love for God and his Word. Now, as we conclude, we hope that this journey has left a deep mark on your heart, igniting a passion for the Living Word.

We would love to hear from you! As the authors of this book, we take great joy in knowing that you have grown closer to the

Life-Giver through this study. Your feedback, testimonies, and journeys have been a source of encouragement and inspiration to us. If this book has played a role in deepening your relationship with the Life-Giver, we rejoice with you and celebrate the work of His Spirit in your life. Please reach out and write to us about your experience. May you continue to find comfort, strength, and wisdom in the Living Word as you seek to know Him more intimately.

Zane and Ruth Darland

ENDNOTES

1   Jon Collins and Tim Mackie, "What is the Story of the Bible?" May 26, 2017, in *The Bible Project Podcast*, produced by The Bible Project, PDF transcript, 59:39, https://d1bsmz3sdihplr.cloudfront. net/media/Podcast%20Transcripts/TBP%20Transcripts/H2R%20 P3%20-%20What%20is%20the%20Story%20of%20the%20Bible%20 Transcript.pdf.

2   Tim Mackie, "Compelled: Speaking and Living the Gospel," Tim Mackie Archives, June 7, 2015, YouTube video, 44:44, https://www. youtube.com/watch?v=qwNfH_SOWKA.

    Tim Mackie, "The First Five Books of the Bible Pentateuch Torah Part 1," Vincent Artale Jr., November 9, 2019, YouTube video, 1:25:30, https://www.youtube.com/watch?v=u8Th_wCfmTo.

3   Ibid.

4   One of the most common and generic names for God in the Bible is Elohim. In Hebrew, this is a plural word, but when used for God, it is

used with a singular verb. A plural being who is singular? The Trinity of God (Father, Son, and Holy Spirit) will continue to be developed throughout the biblical story and become more explicit in the New Testament with the teachings of Jesus and the apostles.

5   Ellen Curtin, "7 Blood-Soaked Facts about the Colosseum," January 14, 2020, https://darkrome.com/blog/Rome/7-bloody-colosseum-facts.

6   Online Etymology Dictionary, s.v. "Arena (n.)," accessed July 10, 2022, https://www.etymonline.com/word/arena.

7   However, as much I desire to give my children the 'best' gifts, I know in our current fallen state, often what they perceive as best and what I know will help bring them to the 'best' place with Jesus are often not the same. As much as God desires to bless us, sometimes in His infinite wisdom, he knows we can't handle it without losing our ultimate focus on Him and living a life that reflects His character.

8   W. E. Vine, Merrill F. Unger, and William White, *Vine's Complete Expository Dictionary of Old and New Testament Words* (Nashville: Thomas Nelson, 1996), 244.

9   Ibid.

10   Daniel R. Jennings, "The Average Life Expectancy of a Porn Star," accessed April 10, 2023, http://danielrjennings.org/TheAverageLifeExpectancyOfAPornStar.html.

     "Porn Industry Reeling," News Corp Australia Network, January 28, 2018, https://www.news.com.au/lifestyle/real-life/news-life/porn-industry-reeling-after-five-deaths-in-only-three-months/news-story/e779587b387f0ad2b3ae71ec45f0c631.

11   "Do We Become More Authentic as We Get Older?" BPS, April 13, 2018, https://www.bps.org.uk/news-and-policy/do-we-become-more-authentic-we-get-older.

12   Thomas Talbott, "Heaven and Hell in Christian Thought," *Stanford Encyclopedia of Philosophy*, last modified February 20, 2021, https://plato.stanford.edu/entries/heaven-hell.

13   Mackie, "Compelled: Speaking and Living the Gospel."

14 Wilbur Glenn Williams, *Genesis: A Commentary for Bible Students* (Indianapolis, IN: Wesleyan Publishing House, 1999), 92.

15 Lee Haines, "The Book of Genesis," in *Genesis-Deuteronomy*, Vol. 1:1, The Wesleyan Bible Commentary (Grand Rapids, MI: William B. Eerdmans Publishing Company, 1967), 45.

16 "The Distinction Between Clean and Unclean Animals," *Ministry Magazine*, January 1968, https://www.ministrymagazine.org/archive/1968/01/the-distinction-between-clean-and-unclean-animals

17 Mackie, "Compelled: Speaking and Living the Gospel."

18 Ibid.

19 "Statistics," Survivors Fund, September 18, 2018, https://survivors-fund.org.uk/learn/statistics.

20 Ibid.

21 *The Dark Tower* by CS Lewis © copyright 1977 CS Lewis Pte Ltd. Used with permission.

22 Ibid.

23 See also 1 Samuel 15:22, Proverbs 21:3, Micah 6:6-8, and Hosea 6:6.

24 Michigan State University, "Animal Legal and Historical Center," accessed July, 12, 2023, https://www.animallaw.info.

   The Humane Society of the United States, "Animal cruelty and human violence FAQ," accessed June 15, 2021, https://www.humanesociety.org/resources/animal-cruelty-and-human-violence-faq.

25 Len Moisan, "Covenants and Contracts are They Different?" The Covenant Group, May 12, 2017, https://covenantgrouponline.com/2017/05/covenants-and-contracts-are-they-different.

26 Whitney Woollard, "Covenants: The Backbone of the Bible," BibleProject, 2019, https://bibleproject.com/blog/covenants-the-backbone-bible.

27 Ibid.

28 Carl Friedrich Keil and Franz Delitzsch, *Commentary on the Old Testament*, Vol. 1. (Peabody, MA: Hendrickson, 1996) p. 105.

29 Kurt Strassner, *Opening up Genesis* (Leominster, England: Day One Publications, 2009) p. 53.

30 James Strong, *A Concise Dictionary of the Words in the Greek Testament and the Hebrew Bible* (Bellingham, WA: Logos Bible Software, 2009), p. 18.

31 BibleProject, "The Way of the Exile," BibleProject, November 1, 2018, YouTube video, https://www.youtube.com/watch?v=XzWpa0gcPyo.

32 James E. Smith, *The Pentateuch*, 2nd ed. (Joplin, MO: College Press Pub. Co., 1993), p. 114.

33 Mackie, "Compelled: Speaking and Living the Gospel."

34 Ed Stetzer, L. F. Cardoso, and E. S. Laxton, "3 Ways Suffering Produces Sanctification," The Exchange, June 2016, https://www.christianitytoday.com/edstetzer/2016/june/3-ways-suffering-produces-sanctification.html.

35 Strassner, Opening up Genesis, p. 71.

36 John H. Walton, Victor H. Matthews, and Mark W. Chavalas, *The IVP Bible Background Commentary: Old Testament* (Downers Grove, InterVarsity Press, 2000), Gen. 15:9-10.

37 See Hebrews 6:18.

38 James McKeown, *Genesis* (Grand Rapids, MI: William B. Eerdmans Publishing Company, 2008), p. 95.

39 See Hebrews 11:12.

40 Robert L. Thomas, *New American Standard Hebrew-Aramaic and Greek Dictionaries: Updated Edition* (La Habra, CA: Lockman Foundation, 1998), #87.

41 Strong, *A Concise Dictionary of the Words in the Greek Testament and The Hebrew Bible*, p. 8.

42 See 1 Corinthians 15:33.

43 James Strong, *Enhanced Strong's Lexicon* (Bellingham, WA: Logos Bible Software, 1995), #40.

44 John Day, "Canaan, Religion of" in David Noel Freedman (Ed.), *The Anchor Yale Bible Dictionary*, Vol. 1 (New York: Doubleday, 1992) p. 834.

45 *The New King James Version* (Nashville: Thomas Nelson, 1982), Gen. 22:14.

46 See Hebrews 11:11b

47 Walter Brueggemann, *Genesis* (Louisville, KY: John Knox Press, 1982), p. 195.

48 Walton, Matthews, and Chavalas, *The IVP Bible Background Commentary: Old Testament*, Gen. 23:14

49 James M. Freeman, *The New Manners & Customs of the Bible* (Gainesville, FL: Bridge-Logos Publishers, 1998) p. 41.

50 Herbert E. Ryle, *The Book of Genesis in the Revised Version with Introduction and Notes* (Cambridge: Cambridge University Press, 1921), p. 263.

51 Strong, *A Concise Dictionary of the Words in the Greek Testament and The Hebrew Bible*, 51.

52 W. Gesenius and Samuel P. Tregelles, *Gesenius' Hebrew and Chaldee Lexicon to the Old Testament Scriptures* (Bellingham, WA: Logos Bible Software, 2003), 865.

53 Bayard Taylor and Gary S. Greig, *The Life of Jesus: His Life, Death, Resurrection and Ministry* (Ventura, CA: Gospel Light, 2011), pp. 113-114.

54 Gesenius and Tregelles, *Gesenius' Hebrew and Chaldee Lexicon to the Old Testament Scriptures*, p. 6.

55 John Gill, *An Exposition of the Old Testament*, vol. 1. (London: Mathews and Leigh, 1810), p. 197.

56 Paul R. Gilchrist, "Judah" in R. Laird Harris, Gleason L. Archer Jr., and Bruce K. Waltke (Eds.), *Theological Wordbook of the Old Testament* (Chicago: Moody Press, 1999), p. 369.

57 John M'Clintock and James Strong, "Dan" in *Cyclopædia of Biblical, Theological, and Ecclesiastical Literature*, Vol. 2. (New York: Harper & Brothers Publishers, 1891), p. 653.

58 Judson Cornwall and Stelman Smith, "Gad" in *The Exhaustive Dictionary of Bible Names* (Gainsville, FL: Bridge-Logos, 1998), p. 75.

59 Gesenius and Tregelles, *Gesenius' Hebrew and Chaldee Lexicon to the Old Testament Scriptures*, p. 343.

60 John E. Hartley, *Genesis* (Grand Rapids, MI: Baker Books, 2012), p. 273.

61 Strong, *A Concise Dictionary of the Words in the Greek Testament and The Hebrew Bible*, vol. 2, p. 95

62 See Deuteronomy 23:7.

63 Cornwall & Smith, "Gad" in *The Exhaustive Dictionary of Bible Names*, p. 75.

64 Lee Haines, "The Book of Genesis" in *Genesis-Deuteronomy*, vol. 1:1 (Grand Rapids, MI: William B. Eerdmans Publishing Company, 1967), p. 125.

65 Sarah Shectman, "Themes and Perspectives in Torah: Creation, Kinship, and Covenant" in Gale A. Yee, Hugh R. Page, Jr., & Matthew J. M. Coomber (Eds.), *The Old Testament and Apocrypha* (Minneapolis: Fortress Press, 2014), p. 261.

66 B. R. Downer & R. K. Harrison, "Cupbearer" in G. W. Bromiley (Ed.), *The International Standard Bible Encyclopedia*, Revised, Vol. 1. (Grand Rapids, MI: William B. Eerdmans Publishing, 1988), p. 837.

67 J. Nkansah-Obrempong, "Dreams" in William A. Dyrness & Veli-Matti Kärkkäinen (Eds.), *Global Dictionary of Theology: A Resource for the Worldwide Church* (Downers Grove, IL: IVP Academic, 2008), p. 241.

68 Nancy L. DeClaissé-Walford, "Asenath" in David Noel Freedman, Allen C. Myers, and Astrid B. Beck (Eds.), *Eerdmans Dictionary of the Bible* (Grand Rapids, MI: William B. Eerdmans Publishing Company, 2000), p. 111.

69 M'Clintock & Strong, *Cyclopædia of Biblical, Theological, and Ecclesiastical Literature*, p. 689.

70 Ibid., 250.

71 Thomas, *New American Standard Hebrew-Aramaic and Greek Dictionaries: Updated Edition*, #6847.

72 See Luke 22:61.

73 See 2 Corinthians 7:10.

74 See Genesis 12:21.

75 See Romans 8:28.

76 See Genesis 45:27.

77 David Guzik, *Enduring Word Bible Commentary* (Enduring Word, 2018), Genesis 46. https://enduringword.com/bible-commentary/genesis-46/.

78 DeClaissé-Walford, *Eerdmans Dictionary of the Bible*, p. 111.

79 Jonathan Rosenberg, "The Numbers in Numbers," 2021, accessed July 13, 2023, https://www.math.umd.edu/~jmr/numbers.html.

80 See Joshua 19:9.

81 See Exodus 32:28.

82 See Joshua 19:10-16.

83 William Ewing, "Gad" in G. W. Bromiley (Ed.), *The International Standard Bible Encyclopedia*, Revised, Vol. 2. (Grand Rapids, MI: William B. Eerdmans Publishing, 1988), p. 374.

84 Jewish Treats, "The Tribe of Asher," NJOP, January 31, 2013, https://njop.org/the-tribe-of-asher/.

85 See Matthew 4:14-15

86 William Ewing and A. A. Saarisalo, "Benjamin" in G. W. Bromiley (Ed.), *The International Standard Bible Encyclopedia*, Revised, Vol. 1. (Grand Rapids, MI: William B. Eerdmans Publishing, 1988), p. 460.

87 Joyce G. Baldwin, *The Message of Genesis 12–50: From Abraham to Joseph* (Nottingham, England: Inter-Varsity Press, 1986), p. 215.

Printed in the United States
by Baker & Taylor Publisher Services